DUMP CAKES
FROM SCRATCH

Nearly 100 Recipes to Dump, Bake, and Devour

JENNIFER LEE

Race Point
PUBLISHING

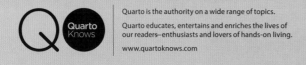

Quarto is the authority on a wide range of topics.

Quarto educates, entertains and enriches the lives of
our readers—enthusiasts and lovers of hands-on living.

www.quartoknows.com

First published in the United States of America in 2016 by
Race Point Publishing, a member of
Quarto Publishing Group USA Inc.
142 West 36th Street, 4th Floor
New York, New York 10018
www.quartoknows.com

10 9 8 7 6 5 4 3 2 1

ISBN 978-1-63106-255-1

Library of Congress Cataloging-in-Publication Data

Names: Lee, Jennifer, 1981- author.
Title: Dump Cakes From Scratch : nearly 100 recipes to dump, bake, and devour
  / Jennifer Lee.
Description: New York, New York : Race Point Publishing, [2016]
Identifiers: LCCN 2016009878 | ISBN 9781631062551 (flexibound)
Subjects: LCSH: Cobblers (Cooking) | LCGFT: Cookbooks.
Classification: LCC TX773 .L414 2016 | DDC 641.86/52--dc23 LC record available at
https://lccn.loc.gov/2016009878

Photography: Meade + Meade Photography
Food Styling: JMS Media
Editorial Director: Jeannine Dillon
Managing Editor: Erin Canning
Project Editor: Jason Chappell
Cover and Interior Design: Jacqui Caulton

Printed in China

CONTENTS

INTRODUCTION

WHAT ARE DUMP CAKES?

What if I told you that you could make a dessert just by dumping a bunch of ingredients into a pan and baking it? No need to get out your mixer and mixing bowls. You'd probably be much more willing to make it than a regular mix cake, right? Well, this is essentially the process of making a dump cake.

This book shares nearly 100 recipes and gives dump cakes a modern-day makeover, allowing you to make desserts *from scratch*.

The traditional dump cake consists of cake mix, canned pie filling, and butter, with the end result resembling a fruit crumble. It's an easy solution, though not necessarily a dessert you should be making often, especially when you think about all the sugar and preservatives that are contained in cake mix and pie filling.

DUMP CAKES MAKEOVER

This book is different. Each recipe provides you with an option to make nearly everything from scratch—allowing you control over the amount of sugar, eliminating many artificial ingredients, and giving you a dessert that tastes completely homemade without that distinct cake-mix flavor. But if you prefer, you can still make the recipes with cake mix and/or canned pie filling.

Two years ago, I wrote *5-Minute Mug Cakes*. One of the reasons I believe that book was so successful was that I took a very different approach to my mug cakes recipes, eliminating the eggy flavor, abundant calories, and other common complaints for mug cakes. I aim to do the same with dump cakes.

While dump cakes can be fun, many people complain about over-the-top sweetness, lumps of uncooked cake mix, and recipes that still require you to stir and mix ingredients before dumping them—in addition to all of those artificial flavors and preservatives. In developing this book, I've tested dozens of methods for making dump cakes. I've tried varying the amounts of cake mix, methods of distributing the butter, ingredients to moisten the cake mix, baking times, baking temperature, etc. I wanted to create a dessert that would evoke more than an "it's good for what it is" type of response—one that could become a beloved recipe, passed down for generations, and shared at gatherings of family and friends.

So whether you're looking for an easy dessert to bring to a party or for the next project to do with your kids, these dump cakes are the answer. Enjoy!

DUMP CAKES 101

WHY DO DUMP CAKES WORK?

Nearly every baking recipe out there calls for mixing. So how is it that you can make a dessert without doing that? Well, the key is achieving the right balance of dry and wet ingredients. The reason why the classic dump cake involves a fruit-filled bottom followed by a layer of cake mix and then butter is that both the fruit and butter help to bake the cake mix. You'll notice that the fruit layer will bubble as it cooks, and as a result, it will also cook any cake mix it touches. The butter layer gives the fat content the cake needs.

DUMP CAKES MADE FROM SCRATCH

While it's true that making a dump cake from scratch involves a little more effort than just opening a mix or a can, it's not that much more effort. For example, blueberry pie filling can be made from scratch with just blueberries, sugar, and cornstarch. So instead of opening a can of pie filling and dumping it, you dump in three ingredients. It's a few more minutes of preparation, but it's still pretty easy and you eliminate a lot of preservatives and sugar, while gaining the health benefits of fresh fruit.

This book also provides recipes for cake mixes from scratch that can be made in advance and stored for up to three months. If you need to make your recipe now and haven't prepared one of these mixes ahead of time, you have the option to use the box cake mix, choose a recipe that doesn't even require a cake mix, or make your mix from scratch right before you make your cake. It's just a few ingredients that you need to stir together!

Like pie filling, there are many advantages to using a cake mix made from scratch. For one thing, your final cake will taste homemade. Box cake mix, whether you love or hate it, has a very distinct flavor. Also, if you've ever checked the ingredients list, you may have been surprised to find all sorts of ingredients you don't even recognize. A basic cake mix made from scratch only needs a handful of dry ingredients—flour, sugar, and leavening agent—and you aren't ingesting all those other less-desirable ingredients in the box mix.

COMMON PROBLEMS SOLVED

Traditional dump cakes are too sweet. Think about it. For a regular cake, you usually add eggs, water, and other ingredients to your cake mix. When you make dump cakes, however, you don't add those extra ingredients so the cake mix is very concentrated—and sweet. Canned pie filling is also very sweet and is added to the already-concentrated cake mix. Other than butter, there's really nothing in a classic dump cake to balance out the sweetness.

I solve this problem in several ways. First, my recipes use less cake mix, about half the amount in a typical box cake mix (traditional dump cakes require you to use the entire box). I also use a homemade filling and homemade cake mix. By making your own cake mix and fruit fillings, you can control the level of sweetness and tailor it to your personal preferences.

Traditional dump cakes leave patches of uncooked cake mix when finished. Since there is generally no mixing and stirring of ingredients, one of the most common problems of dump cakes is that there can be uneven patches of cake mix that don't get cooked, which makes your final cake look very unappetizing.

To solve this, my dump cake recipes use less cake mix. A thin layer is spread across your pan, ensuring that all of the cake mix gets cooked. I also check on the cake about two-thirds of the way through the baking time, so that any uncooked cake mix spots can be pushed into the bubbling mixture, which ensures the finished product is evenly cooked. Slices of butter also help to provide even cooking. Some dump cakes call for poured melted butter or poured soda, but I found that slices of butter placed evenly across the top achieved the best results.

Some dump cake recipes require mixing and stirring. When I first forayed into the world of dump cakes, I was surprised by the number of recipes that called for cake mix to be prepared according to the package instructions, or mixed with milk, yogurt, etc. To me, this was no different than making a regular cake, thus defeating the easy appeal of dump cakes. Even though stirring and mixing could lead to many, many more recipes, they are no longer dump cake recipes. In this book, none of recipes will require you to get out your mixer or stir a bunch of ingredients together (with the exception of the cake mixes made from scratch and toppings, of course).

BEYOND FRUIT

When I was first introduced to dump cakes, I fell in love with the concept. But after a while, I noticed that nearly every recipe I found was the same: Start with some variety of fruit filling; add cake mix; add butter. As much as I enjoy a warm cobbler, I felt like there had to be a way to make other types of dump cakes. Every once in a while, I would excitedly come across a dump cake recipe without that fruit bottom, such as a chocolate cake. But when I read the recipe, it basically would require you to get out a mixing bowl, mix a bunch of ingredients with the cake mix, and then dump it and cook it. In other words, the same process as making a regular cake!

After many, many trials, I was finally able to create dump dessert variations beyond the classic fruit dump cake. In this book, you'll find recipes that taste like brownies, cookies, and even regular cake. These recipes will require a little extra help because they don't have that fruit layer, but they're still easier than having to whisk together several ingredients or use your mixer. These desserts won't be as tall as a standard cake or as thick as a classic brownie or cookie, but they will taste like cake, brownies, and cookies. They are quite delicious and perfect for those craving something without a fruit filling.

INGREDIENTS

All-purpose flour

The majority of recipes in this book use all-purpose flour (often referred to as *plain flour*), which is a type of wheat flour with a medium amount of proteins.

Wheat flours (all-purpose, cake flour, and bread flour) are distinguished by the level of proteins contained in them. As a result, you cannot substitute flours without having to tweak other ingredients in the recipe.

Most of the cake mixes in this book use all-purpose flour since it is the most common flour in people's kitchens. All-purpose flour is usually sold in two varieties: bleached or unbleached. Either one will work for the recipes in this book.

Baking powder and baking soda

The majority of cake mixes use baking powder and/or baking soda. Both baking powder and baking soda are leavening agents, producing carbon dioxide, which allows the baked goods to rise. Make sure your baking powder and baking soda are fresh and stored in a cool, dry space. Once opened, they need to be replaced every few months or they lose their effectiveness. I always write the date I open it on the canister to remind me when it's time to switch it out. If your cake is coming out hard and dense, it's likely that the baking powder or baking soda needs to be replaced. Also, if you plan on storing your from-scratch cake mix for a while, make sure to use the freshest baking powder and baking soda you can.

People often confuse baking powder with baking soda. While both are leavening agents, **they are not interchangeable**! Baking soda is sodium bicarbonate: It needs an acidic ingredient to interact with before it will release carbon dioxide. In the cake mix recipes, baking soda is used in the chocolate versions and the cocoa powder is the acidic ingredient that interacts and triggers the release of carbon dioxide. Baking powder is part sodium bicarbonate already mixed with an acidic element and a starch. It does not need a separate ingredient to react with.

Cake mix

Nearly every recipe in this book calls for cake mix. Homemade cake mixes from scratch are provided on pages 18–21. These can be made ahead of time and stored. If you prefer, you can also use box cake mix. Just do a direct 1:1 substitute. For example, if the recipe calls for 2 cups (320 g) of white cake mix, substitute 2 cups (320 g) of box white cake mix.

Chilled, unsalted butter

All the recipes using butter call for unsalted butter (the one exception is the salted caramel sauce) because salted butters have varying amounts of salt depending on the manufacturer, which can alter the taste of your baked goods. Unsalted butter gives you control over the salt content of your dessert.

For recipes that require sliced butter, I recommend that the butter be kept chilled until you are ready to cut it. You will be slicing the butter into very thin slices, which is easier to do when the butter is cold than when it has softened to room temperature. If you've come across other dump cake recipes, sometimes you'll see that they use melted butter. I tried that method several times but found that the butter did not spread as evenly across the cake, which is why I use the butter slices method. (There are a few recipes that are not traditional dump cakes that do require melted butter.)

Cornstarch

Cornstarch is used two ways in most of the recipes in this book.

First, it's used in the cake mix itself. In baked goods, cornstarch helps create a tender crumb. If you've ever had a cake made with cake flour, you'll notice that it's airier and more delicate than a cake baked with all-purpose flour. This is because cake flour has fewer proteins, which means that less gluten forms when you are mixing it, so baked goods stay lighter. The cornstarch softens the proteins, mimicking the protein levels of cake flour. (This is also why cornstarch is often mixed with all-purpose flour as a cake flour substitute.)

Second, it's used in the fruit filling as a thickening agent, so that the fruit filling becomes like a pie filling.

Dutch process cocoa powder, unsweetened

The chocolate cake mixes in this book use unsweetened Dutch process cocoa powder. This refers to baking cocoa powder as opposed to drinking cocoa powder. Unsweetened cocoa powder usually comes in two forms: natural and Dutch process.

Dutch process, or alkalized, cocoa powder has been treated with an alkalizing agent to reduce the acidity of the cocoa. It's usually darker in color, and is labeled something along the lines like "Dutched," "Dutch-processed," or "processed with alkali." This type of cocoa powder is sometimes found at supermarkets, but may need to be purchased at baking supply stores.

Natural cocoa is usually lighter in color and has not had its acid removed. It is often labeled "natural." This is the most common type of unsweetened cocoa found at supermarkets produced by popular brands like Hershey's and Ghirardelli.

Fat-free milk powder

Many of my from-scratch cake mixes call for milk powder, which is readily available at most grocery stores. While a basic cake mix is just sugar, baking powder, and flour, the milk powder helps keep the cake moist and fluffy. You know how most box cake mix brands advertise that instant pudding mix has been added to the cake mix? Well, it's basically the same idea. The milk powder and cornstarch are a substitute for the instant pudding mix.

Fruit

For these recipes, you can use fruit that is fresh, frozen, or canned—or pie filling. My favorite is frozen. Frozen fruit is healthy, doesn't have added sugar, and is already washed and cut, which reduces preparation time. For all the recipes that contain a fruit bottom, you can substitute other forms of fruit, as long as you make the following modifications:

For frozen fruit, use the fruit in its frozen state, letting it defrost while baking. If you want to use frozen fruit in a recipe that calls for fresh fruit, use twice the amount of cornstarch required in the recipe.

For fresh fruit, make sure to wash and dry your fruit before using. If you are using fresh fruit in a recipe that calls for frozen fruit, reduce the amount of cornstarch in the recipe by half. If your fresh fruit isn't as sweet as that type of fruit usually is, add a few extra tablespoons of sugar to compensate.

For canned fruit, I recommend buying canned fruit that is preserved in its own juice rather than in syrup. If you are using canned fruit in a recipe that calls for frozen or fresh fruit, measure the fruit without the juice. Reserve 2 tablespoons juice for every 1 cup fruit. Add both the reserved juice and fruit into your recipe. Use the same amount of cornstarch, but reduce the sugar by half.

For pie filling, replace the same amount of fruit required with pie filling, but omit the sugar and cornstarch.

Granulated white sugar

This is the most common sugar found in people's pantries and used for cooking—often referred to as *regular sugar*, *white sugar*, or *table sugar*.

Feel free to increase or reduce the amount of granulated sugar in each recipe to suit your personal preferences. However, please do not change the amount or type of sugar in the from-scratch mixes or syrups as it may affect the balance and structure of your desserts.

Ice cream

A handful of recipes use ice cream in the actual dessert. Make sure you use a full-fat ice cream that contains eggs. The ingredients in the ice cream help create structure for the cake.

Any of these desserts can be also served with ice cream, especially the warm crumbles, cobblers, and crisps. When used as a topping, you can use your favorite ice cream brand and flavor.

Lemon-lime soda

A few recipes require the addition of lemon-lime soda. Popular brands are Sprite or 7-Up. I specify lemon-lime because it has a more neutral flavor and you won't be able to detect the lemon-lime once it is cooked in the cake. Make sure the soda has not gone flat as the recipe requires the carbonation.

If you prefer not to use soda, I've provided a homemade alternative on page 173 in the Mix-Ins and Toppings from Scratch chapter, using club soda and sugar. It's not the same as a commercial soda, nor is it a homemade soda recipe, but it's a quick fix that mimics the effects of soda for the purposes of the recipe.

Light brown sugar

Brown sugar is granulated sugar with molasses. Light brown sugar has a golden color and mild molasses flavor. Dark brown sugar has a darker brown hue and a richer molasses flavor. The recipes in this book that use brown sugar call for light brown sugar (with the exception of the dulce de leche sauce). If you only have dark brown sugar at home, you can substitute it for light brown, but know that your cake will have a deeper molasses flavor.

Brown sugar will sometimes harden into lumps. If that happens, you can heat it up in the microwave for a few seconds to make it moist again.

Powdered sugar

Powdered sugar, or confectioners' sugar, is granulated sugar that has been ground to a smooth powder. It's often used to make frostings because it dissolves more easily than granulated sugar.

EQUIPMENT

Baking pans

The majority of the recipes in this book are made in either a standard 9 × 13 × 2-inch (23 × 33 × 5 cm) rectangular baking pan (referred to as a "9 × 13-inch baking pan") or a 9 × 9 × 1½-inch (23 × 23 × 4 cm) square baking pan (referred to as a "9 × 9-inch baking pan").

A few recipes call for the use of a round baking dish 5 to 5 ½ inches (12.7 cm to 14 cm) in diameter and at least 2 inches (5 cm) tall. There are several different kinds of pans that fit this description, such as small spring form cake pans, small pie pans, mini casserole dishes, or gratin bowls. Just make sure they are oven-safe and as close to the dimensions listed as possible. If your pan is too narrow, your cake won't cook evenly. If it's too wide, your cake will come out too thin.

Liquid and dry measuring cups

If you are using cup measurements to make these recipes, please make sure to use liquid measuring cups to measure liquids and dry measuring cups to measure dry ingredients. While both liquid and dry measuring cups hold the same volume, they are designed differently so that you can most accurately measure your respective ingredients.

Liquid measuring cups usually have several measurements on the side of the cup, with lines to indicate where to measure to, along with a spout for easy pouring. Dry measuring cups have separate cups for each of the measurements they correspond to.

If you attempt to measure a liquid in a dry measuring cup, you'll have to fill the cup to the very brim to get the most accurate measurement. This is quite tricky and you'll likely spill some of the liquid before you are able to empty your cup into the baking pan. Accurately measuring dry ingredients in liquid measuring cups is even more difficult. When you measure dry ingredients in a dry cup, you simply fill to the top and then level it off. Liquid measurement cups have measurement lines located below the top of the cup so that you don't need to fill all of the way to the top and risk spilling. However, this makes it difficult to level your dry ingredients for an accurate measurement.

Parchment paper

As discussed in the Baking Process section, baking pans can be lined with parchment paper. Parchment paper is a nonstick, heat-resistant paper specially treated for oven use.

Parchment paper is sometimes confused with wax paper, which has a similar appearance and is also nonstick. Please do not use wax paper in place of parchment paper when baking! Wax paper is not meant to withstand high heat.

Sifter

A few of the nontraditional dump cakes in this book require you to sift in the homemade cake mix. If you own a flour sifter, great! If not, don't worry. A regular mesh strainer will work just fine and it is what I use.

BAKING PROCESS

Measuring ingredients

Dry ingredients. In general, to measure dry ingredients, spoon your ingredient into your corresponding dry measuring cup and then level it off with a straight edge, like the non-ridged edge of a butter knife. For very small quantities of dry ingredients like tablespoons or teaspoons, simply use that corresponding measuring spoon to do the scooping and make sure to level off with a straight edge for the most accurate measurement.

A common mistake often occurs when measuring flour. Be careful not to "pack" it. Packing occurs when you scoop the flour directly from the bag into your measuring cup—this results in too much flour in the cup and will make your cakes dry and tough. To measure your flour, first spoon it into your measuring spoon or cup and then level it off with a knife.

Similarly, make sure not to "pack" your cake mix.

Brown sugar. Unlike most dry ingredients, you do want brown sugar to be packed when you measure it. To do so, scoop your measuring device directly into the brown sugar container, adding in a little more than the cup or spoon can hold. Then use your fingers to lightly press the sugar down, and level off with a knife if needed. When you turn out the brown sugar, it should hold the shape of the cup or spoon.

Fruit. Measuring fruit can be a little tricky. The different shapes and sizes make fruit difficult to properly stack into a measuring cup. To measure the fruit quantities for the recipes in this book, use a dry measuring cup that corresponds to the measurement required and fill your cup a little above the brim. While you want to be as accurate as you can for all ingredients, the fruit measurement is a little more forgiving, so it's okay to be a little over.

Greasing or lining baking pans

There are two methods for preparing your baking pans: greasing or lining with parchment paper. Both methods will prevent the cake from sticking to the pan.

Even if you are using a nonstick baking pan, I recommend that you grease it. The easiest way is to use a cooking oil spray (it does not need to be one that contains flour); simply spray all surfaces inside of your pan. If you don't have a cooking spray or prefer not to use one, you can take some melted butter or vegetable oil and lightly brush the inside of your pan.

You can also line your baking pans with parchment paper cut to fit your pan size. Doing so makes cleanup even faster as your baking pan will be much easier to wash. However, the presentation may not be quite as nice when you have parchment paper sticking out from beneath your cake, so the choice is up to you.

To line your pan, cut the parchment paper to fit the pan, with about one to two inches of overhang on each side. Your parchment paper should completely cover the entire bottom of the pan. Lightly grease the underside of the parchment paper so that it sticks to the pan. Even though parchment paper is nonstick, I recommend that also you grease the surface of the parchment paper, just like you would grease your baking pan. Next, crease and fold the overhang so that it does not get in the way during baking. The overhang is used for easy removal of the cake after baking. Lining your pan makes cleanup simple as your baking pan will be much easier to wash.

Sprinkling cake mix

Most of the recipes in this book require you to sprinkle cake mix evenly across your pan. You can do this simply by dipping your fingers into your cup, picking up a small amount of cake mix, and then rubbing the mix between your fingers into the pan. You can also dip a small spoon into your measuring cup and then shake your wrist side to side to sprinkle the cake mix in.

Sifting cake mix

A few recipes—the ones that don't have a fruit bottom—will require you to sift in the homemade cake mix. This step is key to making sure the cake turns out properly. Sifting eliminates any clumps of cake mix and allows the liquids in the recipe to evenly saturate the dry ingredients. And it will only add about 30 seconds extra to your preparation time.

As discussed in the Equipment section, if you don't own a flour sifter, simply use a mesh food strainer.

First, measure out the required amount of cake mix. Next, fill your mesh strainer about halfway with cake mix and then shake your wrist left and right, hitting the strainer gently against your other hand, to allow the cake mix to sift through the strainer. Repeat with any remaining cake mix.

When you are finished sifting, you may notice some large granules of sugar or milk powder that have gotten stuck at the bottom of your strainer. Simply sprinkle them on top of the sifted cake mix.

Please note, this sifting process is only required for recipes that specify for you to sift the cake mix.

Baking

When baking, the ideal placement for the most even cooking of your cake is usually in the middle of your oven. If you place your cake too close to the top or the bottom, the top or bottom of the cake can finish baking before the other parts of the cake are done.

Because everyone's ovens operate a little differently, baking times are always approximate. Other factors that can greatly affect baking time include cooking other items in your oven at the same time, which affects heat distribution, and opening your oven door, which changes the temperature inside your oven.

Microwave cooking

As with ovens, microwave cooking time can vary depending on your microwave. Microwaves usually range between 700 and 1200 watts. My times are based on my 1000-watt microwave, with the desserts cooked at full power. If your microwave has a lower wattage, please start with the time stated and then add more time as needed. Similarly, if your microwave has a high wattage, start with a slightly shorter amount of time and add time as needed.

Check on cake/Push down cake mix

As I mentioned in the introduction, one of the most common issues with dump cakes is that there are often patches of uncooked cake mix left in the finished cake. To help prevent this from occurring, most of my recipes require you to check on the cake about two-thirds of the way through the baking time and push down any remaining clumps of dry cake mix into the bubbling batter. You can do so with a spatula or large spoon.

Quickly check on the cake. Once you open the oven door, it will cause the temperature inside your oven to drop considerably. Therefore, you want to be as quick and efficient as possible so that your cakes are cooking at the desired temperature for nearly the entire baking time. Most of the recipes ask you to push uncooked cake mix into the bubbling batter. You should first check the progress of your cake by turning on the oven light and peering through the oven window to make sure your cake is bubbling. If it isn't, wait a few more minutes until it is. Then, briefly open your oven door and push down the cake mix (as described in more detail below) with a spatula or large spoon and then quickly close the oven door again as soon as you are finished.

Push down cake mix. For the dump cakes with a fruit bottom, the cakes should be deep enough for you to easily push the cake mix in. You want to push it down until all of it is completely moistened with wet batter. Don't worry if you have to break the surface of already-cooked pieces of cake, as it will smooth out again as it continues to bake.

For the thin dump cakes that don't have as much liquid on the bottom, the goal is just to get the dry cake-mix sections moistened. You can do this by lightly scraping portions of the surface that are already wet and bubbling and gently spreading that across the dry surface. I like to think of it like spreading butter on toast. As long as the dry cake mix gets a little bit of the moisture from other parts of the cake, it should cook all the way through.

Slow cookers

Slow cookers are a fun way to make your dump cake desserts without having to continually check on them. You just set your slow cooker and then let it do the work. If you own a programmable slow cooker, when the cake is done, it'll just stay in warm mode until you are ready to eat.

Because of the slow cooking method, the tops of the cakes won't be as crunchy as when they're baked in the oven. However, they will still have a nice, solid, buttery crumble.

The slow cooker recipes are based on my 6-quart (5.7 L) slow cooker. If you have a smaller slow cooker, please adjust ingredient measurements and cooking times as needed.

Storing cake mix

The from-scratch cake mixes in this book can be made ahead of time and stored in a sealed container in a cool, dark place. Because this cake mix does not contain preservatives, it will not have as long a shelf life as box cake mix. I recommend that the cake mixes be used within three months. This recommendation is based on the assumption that all the individual ingredients contained within the cake mix have at least a three-month shelf life left. For instance, if you use milk powder that is set to expire in one month, then make sure you use your cake mix within one month. I recommend writing the date on the outside of the container so you remember when to use to use your mix by.

CHOCOLATE CAKE MIX

1¾ cups (220 g) all-purpose flour

1½ teaspoons (7.5 ml) baking powder

1½ teaspoons (7.5 ml) baking soda

1¾ cups (350 g) granulated white sugar

½ cup (48 g) unsweetened Dutch process cocoa powder

2 tablespoons (30 ml) cornstarch

Yields approximately 4 cups (620 g) of cake mix

Combine all ingredients in a large mixing bowl. Stir with a whisk until well mixed (about 40–50 strokes), making sure to occasionally lift and run the whisk along the sides of the bowl so that all ingredients are fully incorporated. If your cocoa powder has clumps even after whisking, pour your cake mix into a food processor and pulse a few times until the clumps disappear. Store in an airtight container in your pantry (or other cool, dark space) for up to three months, assuming all of the individual ingredients used have a shelf life longer than three months. If anything has a shorter shelf life, use your mix by the shortest shelf-life date.

FUNFETTI CAKE MIX

———— •• ————

2 cups (250 g) all-purpose flour

1 tablespoon (15 ml) baking powder

1½ cups (300 g) granulated white sugar

½ cup (60 g) nonfat dry milk powder

¼ cup (32 g) cornstarch

1 cup (160 g) rainbow sprinkles

Yields approximately 5 cups (800 g) of cake mix

Combine all ingredients except sprinkles in a large mixing bowl. Stir with a whisk until well mixed (about 20–30 strokes), making sure to occasionally lift and run the whisk along the sides of the bowl so that all ingredients are fully incorporated. Stir in sprinkles. Store in an airtight container in your pantry (or other cool, dark space) for up to three months, assuming all of the individual ingredients used have a shelf life longer than three months. If anything has a shorter shelf life, use your mix by the shortest shelf-life date.

SPICE CAKE MIX

———— •• ————

2 cups (250 g) all-purpose flour

1 tablespoon (15 ml) baking powder

1½ cups (300 g) granulated white sugar

½ cup (60 g) nonfat dry milk powder

¼ cup (32 g) cornstarch

4 teaspoons (20 ml) cinnamon

Yields approximately 4 cups (640 g) of cake mix

Combine all ingredients in a large mixing bowl. Stir with a whisk until well mixed (about 20–30 strokes), making sure to occasionally lift and run the whisk along the sides of the bowl so that all ingredients are fully incorporated. Store in an airtight container in your pantry (or other cool, dark space) for up to three months, assuming all of the individual ingredients used have a shelf life longer than three months. If anything has a shorter shelf life, use your mix by the shortest shelf-life date.

WHITE CAKE MIX

2 cups (250 g) all-purpose flour

1 tablespoon (15 ml) baking powder

1½ cups (300 g) granulated white sugar

½ cup (60 g) nonfat dry milk powder

¼ cup (32 g) cornstarch

Yields approximately 4 cups (640 g) of cake mix

Combine all ingredients in a large mixing bowl. Stir with a whisk until well mixed (about 20–30 strokes), making sure to occasionally lift and run the whisk along the sides of the bowl so that all ingredients are fully incorporated. Store in an airtight container in your pantry (or other cool, dark space) for up to three months, assuming all of the individual ingredients used have a shelf life longer than three months. If anything has a shorter shelf life, use your mix by the shortest shelf-life date.

GLUTEN-FREE WHITE CAKE MIX

2 cups (256g) gluten-free all-purpose flour (see * note opposite)

1 tablespoon (15 ml) baking powder

1½ cups (300 g) granulated white sugar

½ cup (60 g) nonfat dry milk powder

¼ cup (32 g) cornstarch

Yields approximately 4 cups (640 g) of cake mix

Combine all ingredients in a large mixing bowl. Stir with a whisk until well mixed (about 20–30 strokes), making sure to occasionally lift and run the whisk along the sides of the bowl so that all ingredients are fully incorporated. Store in an airtight container in your pantry (or other cool, dark space) for up to three months, assuming all of the individual ingredients used have a shelf life longer than three months. If anything has a shorter shelf life, use your mix by the shortest shelf-life date.

GLUTEN-FREE CHOCOLATE CAKE MIX

——— ◆ ———

1¾ cups (224 g) gluten-free all-purpose flour*

1½ teaspoons (7.5 ml) baking powder

1½ teaspoons (7.5 ml) baking soda

1¾ cups (350 g) granulated white sugar

½ cup (48 g) unsweetened Dutch process cocoa powder

2 tablespoons (30 ml) cornstarch

Yields approximately 4 cups (620 g) of cake mix

Combine all ingredients in a large mixing bowl. Stir with a whisk until well mixed (about 40–50 strokes), making sure to occasionally lift and run the whisk along the sides of the bowl so that all ingredients are fully incorporated. If your cocoa powder has clumps even after whisking, pour your cake mix into a food processor and pulse a few times until the clumps disappear. Store in an airtight container in your pantry (or other cool, dark space) for up to three months, assuming all of the individual ingredients used have a shelf life longer than three months. If anything has a shorter shelf life, use your mix by the shortest shelf-life date.

* *For gluten-free flour, if you have a favorite brand, please use that. If you are unfamiliar with gluten-free flours, I recommend Cup4Cup gluten-free flour, developed in Thomas Keller's The French Laundry restaurant, which can be found online on Amazon and at specialty stores like Williams-Sonoma. I've tested several gluten-free flour brands and found that Cup4Cup yielded results closest to all-purpose flour, with the least amount of that gritty aftertaste you often get with gluten-free baked goods. When I'm unable to get my hands on Cup4Cup, I'll use Bob's Red Mill, which is available at most grocery stores.*

FRUITY DUMP CAKES

Fruit-based dump cakes are the most classic of dump cakes. When baked, the cake mix forms a golden brown, buttery rich crumble over the fruit filling. I encourage you to serve these cakes warm. Top with a scoop of ice cream and a drizzle of fudge or caramel sauce and it's the perfect ending to any meal.

I recommend you start with a recipe in this chapter before exploring other recipes in the book. The recipes in this section will help familiarize you with the process of making dump cakes. Once you get the hang of things, you can move on to other dump cake variations.

Fruity dump cakes can be made year-round. In the summer, they're a great way to use up extra fresh fruit. In the winter, you can switch to frozen or canned fruit. Please make sure to refer to page 11 for how to handle the different forms of fruit before making one of the cakes from this chapter.

CARAMEL APPLE CAKE

Prep time: 15–20 minutes   Cook time: 40–45 minutes

Serves 12–15

I usually don't like playing favorites, but this is one of my favorite recipes in this book. Gooey salted caramel sauce is mixed with soft apples for an indulgent and wonderfully delicious cake. It's a lovely pairing of sweet and salty and a cake I make over and over again. If you're looking for a binge-worthy dessert, this cake is it.

3 cups (450 g) peeled fresh apple cubes, approximately ½-inch (13 mm) cubes

½ cup (120 ml) thick, salted caramel sauce (store bought or see page 171)

2 cups (320 g) White Cake Mix (page 20)

½ cup or 1 stick (4 ounces/113 g) unsalted butter, sliced into ¼-inch-thick (6 mm) squares

1   Preheat oven to 350°F (175°C). Grease or line a 9 × 13-inch (23 × 33 cm) baking pan.

2   Dump and evenly spread apples across pan. Pour caramel sauce over apples.

3   Sprinkle dry cake mix evenly across pan. Spread butter slices evenly across top.

4   Bake for 40–45 minutes. About 30 minutes in, quickly check the cake. Use a spatula or large spoon to push down any uncooked cake mix into the bubbling mixture. Do not worry if this breaks the surface of the cake. Let the cake continue to bake for an additional 10–15 minutes, until the surface is completely golden brown.

5   Let cake cool for about 30 minutes before serving as the fruit layer will be extremely hot. If desired, serve with a scoop of your favorite ice cream and/or any of the toppings provided on pages 168–173.

AUTUMN APPLE CRISP

Prep time: 15–20 minutes   Cook time: 30–35 minutes

Serves 12–15

When the air turns crisp and the leaves change color, I get excited for the start of apple season. As a kid, I would pick bags upon bags of apples from apple orchards. And then I would have to scramble to find various apple recipes because there were just too many to eat! One of my favorite ways to use up apples is in an apple crisp. This apple crisp combines fresh apples with applesauce, which results in a warm, comforting, and saucy apple filling.

1 cup (150 g) peeled fresh apple cubes, approximately ½-inch (13 mm) cubes

1 cup (245 g) unsweetened applesauce

2 cups (320 g) Spice Cake Mix (page 19)

½ cup or 1 stick (4 ounces/ 113 g) unsalted butter, sliced into ¼-inch-thick (6 mm) squares

1 Preheat oven to 350°F (175°C). Grease a 9 × 13-inch (23 × 33 cm) baking pan or line with parchment paper.

2 Dump and evenly spread apples across bottom of pan. Evenly spread applesauce across the pan.

3 Sprinkle dry cake mix evenly across pan. Spread butter slices evenly across top.

4 Bake for 30–35 minutes. About 20 minutes in, quickly check the cake. Use a spatula or large spoon to push down any uncooked cake mix into the bubbling mixture. Do not worry if this breaks the surface of the cake. Let the cake continue to bake for an additional 10–15 minutes, until the surface is completely golden brown.

5 Let cake cool for about 20 minutes before serving as the fruit layer will be extremely hot. If desired, serve with a scoop of your favorite ice cream and/or any of the toppings provided on pages 168–173.

BANANA-ANA CAKE

Prep time: 10–15 minutes   Cook time: 30–35 minutes

Serves 9–12

Is there anything more comforting than warm, homemade banana cake? I don't make it as often as I would like because traditional banana cake involves mashing ugly brown bananas, stirring a bunch of ingredients, pouring everything into a pan, and then baking for about an hour.

This banana dump cake preserves all the flavors of a regular banana cake, but with a much shorter preparation and cook time. It also adds an extra dose of banana flavor since the banana is not mashed up and mixed into the cake batter. I sighed with pleasure when I first tasted this cake—hopefully you'll find it equally as comforting.

2 very ripe medium bananas, peeled and cut into ¼-inch-thick (6 mm) slices

¼ cup (60 g) light brown sugar, packed

1 cup (160 g) Spice Cake Mix (page 19)

¼ cup or ½ stick (2 ounces/57 g) unsalted butter, sliced into ¼-inch-thick (6 mm) squares

1   Preheat oven to 350°F (175°C). Grease or line a 9 × 9-inch (23 × 23 cm) baking pan.

2   Dump and lay banana slices evenly across bottom of pan. You should have enough to line the entire bottom, with the slices side by side and touching, and then enough left over for a more spread-out layer on top.

3   Sprinkle brown sugar evenly across bananas. Then, sprinkle dry cake mix evenly across pan. Spread butter slices evenly across top.

4   Bake for 30–35 minutes. About 20 minutes in, quickly check the cake. Use a spatula or large spoon to push down any uncooked cake mix into the bubbling mixture. Do not worry if this breaks the surface of the cake. Let the cake continue to bake for an additional 10–15 minutes, until the surface is completely golden brown.

5   Let cake cool for about 20–30 minutes before serving as the fruit layer will be extremely hot. If desired, serve with a scoop of your favorite ice cream and/or any of the toppings provided on pages 168–173.

BURSTING BLUEBERRY COBBLER

♦

Prep time: 10–15 minutes   Cook time: 45–50 minutes

Serves 12–15

My very first dump cake was this blueberry cobbler, so it has special meaning for me. I love to make it in the summer, when blueberries are super sweet and plump. If you've just gone blueberry picking and are looking for a way to use up berries, this recipe requires a whopping four cups. But if you're like me, I am always reluctant to part with so many delicious fresh berries. I end up doing a game of "one for the cake and one for me" and then I run out of berries! As a result, I tend to use frozen blueberries for the bottom fruit layer and fresh berries for the top garnish layer. It's a nice compromise and I really love the way the fresh berry juices run across the top of the buttery cobbler.

3 cups (465 g) frozen blueberries

2 tablespoons (30 ml) cornstarch

¾ cup (150 g) granulated white sugar

2 cups (320 g) White Cake Mix (page 20)

½ cup or 1 stick (4 ounces/113 g) unsalted butter, sliced into ¼-inch-thick (6 mm) squares

1 cup (150 g) fresh blueberries

1   Preheat oven to 350°F (175°C). Grease or line a 9 × 13-inch (23 × 33 cm) baking pan.

2   Dump and evenly spread frozen blueberries across pan. Sprinkle berries with cornstarch, then sugar.

3   Sprinkle dry cake mix evenly across pan. Spread butter slices evenly on top of cake mix. Scatter fresh blueberries on top.

4   Bake for 45–50 minutes. About 30 minutes in, quickly check the cake. Use a spatula or large spoon to push down any uncooked cake mix into the bubbling mixture. Do not worry if this breaks the surface of the cake. Let the cake continue to bake for an additional 15–20 minutes, until the surface is completely golden brown.

5   Let cake cool for about 30 minutes before serving as the fruit layer will be extremely hot. If desired, serve with a scoop of your favorite ice cream and/or any of the toppings provided on pages 168–173.

PEACHES AND CREAM COBBLER

Prep time: 10–15 minutes   Cook time: 40–45 minutes

Serves 9–12

Peaches and cream is a favorite summertime dessert of mine. For a fun take on the classic, this cobbler is filled with sliced peaches and sweet cooked cream and topped with a golden, buttery crust. I suggest you serve it with fresh whipped cream to make it really taste like the original.

2 cups (500 g) frozen peach slices

1 tablespoon (15 ml) cornstarch

½ cup (100 g) granulated white sugar

¼ cup (60 ml) heavy cream

1 cup (160 g) White Cake Mix (page 20)

2 tablespoons (1 ounce/28 g) unsalted butter, sliced into ¼-inch-thick (6 mm) squares

1   Preheat oven to 350°F (175°C). Grease or line a 9 × 9-inch (23 × 23 cm) baking pan.

2   Dump and spread peach slices evenly across bottom of pan, making sure the peach slices are lying on their sides. Sprinkle peach slices with cornstarch, then sugar.

3   Pour heavy cream evenly across pan. Then, sprinkle evenly with dry cake mix. Spread butter slices evenly across top.

4   Bake for 40–45 minutes. About 25 minutes in, quickly check the cake. Use a spatula or large wooden spoon to push down any uncooked cake mix into the bubbling mixture. Do not worry if this breaks the surface of the cake. Let the cake continue to bake for an additional 15–20 minutes, until the surface is completely golden brown.

5   Let cake cool for about 20–30 minutes before serving as the fruit layer will be extremely hot. If desired, serve with whipped cream (page 171).

STRAWBERRY PIE BARS

— • • —

Prep time: 15–20 minutes   Cook time: 40–45 minutes

Serves 9–12

Have you ever had a pie bar? They are one of my favorite desserts because they have a double crust—my favorite part of the pie! If I could, I would eat all the crust off a pie and let other people eat the filling. These strawberry pie bars have a thin layer of cake mix crust, followed by a layer of strawberry filling, and then a thicker layer of buttery crumb topping.

1½ cups (240 g) White Cake Mix (page 20), divided

2 tablespoons (1 ounce/28 g), plus ¼ cup or ½ stick (2 ounces/55 g) unsalted butter, sliced into ¼-inch-thick (6 mm) squares, divided

2 cups (340 g) fresh strawberries, hulled and chopped

1½ teaspoons (7.5 ml) cornstarch

½ cup (100 g) granulated white sugar

1 Preheat oven to 350°F (175°C). Grease or line a 9 × 13-inch (23 × 33 cm) baking pan.

2 Sprinkle and evenly spread ½ cup (80 g) dry cake mix across bottom of pan. Place 2 tablespoons butter slices evenly across cake mix. Top with chopped strawberries. Sprinkle strawberries evenly with cornstarch, then sugar.

3 Evenly sprinkle remaining 1 cup (160 g) dry cake mix across top, and top with remaining ¼ cup (57 g) butter slices.

4 Bake for 40–45 minutes. About 30 minutes in, quickly check the cake. Use a spatula or large wooden spoon to push down any uncooked cake mix into the bubbling mixture. Do not worry if this breaks the surface of the cake. Let the cake continue to bake for an additional 10–15 minutes, until the surface is completely golden brown.

5 Let cake cool for about 30 minutes to allow the fruit layer to set, before cutting into bars and serving.

PIÑA COLADA CRUMBLE

Prep time: 10–15 minutes   Cook time: 30–35 minutes

Serves 9–12

With chunks of pineapple, toasted coconut, and a hint of rum, this piña colada cake is like the popular cocktail in cake form. Share it with a bunch of friends for your own at-home happy hour experience.

2 cups (500 g) frozen pineapple chunks

1 tablespoon (15 ml) cornstarch

½ cup (100 g) granulated white sugar

1 cup (160 g) White Cake Mix (page 20)

¼ cup (60 ml) dark rum

1 cup (90 g) sweetened coconut flakes

¼ cup or ½ stick (2 ounces/57 g) unsalted butter, sliced into ¼-inch-thick (16 mm) squares

1   Preheat oven to 350°F (175°C). Grease or line a 9 × 9-inch (23 × 23 cm) baking pan.

2   Dump and spread pineapple chunks evenly across bottom of pan. Sprinkle pineapple with cornstarch, then sugar.

3   Sprinkle dry cake mix evenly across pineapple mixture; then drizzle rum over cake mix. Evenly sprinkle with coconut flakes. Spread butter slices evenly across top.

4   Bake for 30–35 minutes. About 20 minutes in, quickly check the cake. Use a spatula or large spoon to push down any uncooked cake mix into the bubbling mixture. Do not worry if this breaks the surface of the cake. Let the cake continue to bake for an additional 10–15 minutes, until the surface is completely golden brown.

5   Let cake cool for about 20–30 minutes before serving as the fruit layer will be extremely hot. If desired, serve with a scoop of your favorite ice cream and/or any of the toppings provided on pages 168–173.

TROPICAL VACATION CAKE

Prep time: 10–15 minutes   Cook time: 45–50 minutes

Serves 12–16

As much as I'd like to be on vacation all the time, it's just not possible. That doesn't mean I can't pretend I'm somewhere warm, relaxing, and tropical though. With mangoes, pineapples, and coconut, this cake tastes like tropical paradise.

2 cups (500 g) frozen mango chunks

2 cups (500 g) frozen pineapple chunks

2 tablespoons (30 ml) cornstarch

½ cup (100 g) granulated white sugar

2 cups (320 g) White Cake Mix (page 20)

½ cup (45 g) sweetened coconut flakes

½ cup or 1 stick (4 ounces/113 g) unsalted butter, sliced into ¼-inch-thick (6 mm) squares

1   Preheat oven to 350°F (175°C). Grease or line a 9 × 13-inch (23 × 33 cm) baking pan.

2   Dump and evenly spread mango and pineapple chunks in pan. Sprinkle evenly with cornstarch, then sugar.

3   Sprinkle dry cake mix evenly across pan. Spread butter slices evenly across top. Sprinkle coconut flakes across top.

4   Bake for 45–50 minutes. About 30 minutes in, quickly check the cake. Use a spatula or large wooden spoon to push down any uncooked cake mix into the bubbling mixture. Do not worry if this breaks the surface of the cake. Let the cake continue to bake for an additional 15–20 minutes, until the surface is completely golden brown.

5   Let cake cool for about 30 minutes before serving as the fruit layer will be extremely hot. If desired, serve with a scoop of your favorite ice cream and/or any of the toppings provided on pages 168–173.

RASPBERRY CHEESECAKE

Prep time: 10–15 minutes   Cook time: 35–40 minutes

Serves 9–12

I have a hard time resisting a slice of cheesecake when it's offered to me. As you may have already guessed, this isn't your typical cheesecake, but it does capture the essence of the New York cheesecake, in a lighter, fun version that combines the gentle tartness of raspberries with chunks of sweetened cream cheese.

2 cups (250 g) fresh raspberries

½ tablespoon (7.5 ml) cornstarch

½ cup (100 g) granulated white sugar, divided

4 ounces (115 g) cream cheese, cut into very small cubes (½ inch × ½ inch/13 mm × 13 mm)

1 cup (160 g) White Cake Mix (page 20)

¼ cup or ½ stick (2 ounces/ 57 g) unsalted butter, sliced into ¼-inch-thick (6 mm) squares

1. Preheat oven to 350°F (175°C). Grease or line a 9 × 9-inch (23 × 23 cm) baking pan.

2. Dump and evenly spread raspberries across bottom of pan. Sprinkle berries with cornstarch, then with ¼ cup sugar.

3. Place cream cheese cubes evenly across pan and sprinkle with remaining ¼ cup sugar. Sprinkle dry cake mix evenly across mixture. Spread butter slices evenly across top.

4. Bake for 35–40 minutes. About 25–30 minutes in, quickly check the cake. Use a spatula or large spoon to push down any uncooked cake mix into the bubbling mixture. Do not worry if this breaks the surface of the cake. Let the cake continue to bake for approximately 10 minutes more, until the surface is dark golden brown.

5. Let cake cool for about 20–30 minutes before serving as the fruit layer will be extremely hot. If desired, serve with a scoop of your favorite ice cream and/or any of the toppings provided on pages 168–173.

SUPERFRUIT CRISP

———•◆•———

Prep time: 10–15 minutes   Cook time: 45–50 minutes

Serves 12–15

Blueberries, blackberries, and raspberries are all classified as superfruits, packed with anti-oxidants and other health benefits. Luckily for us, the three often come packaged and frozen together. This cake has a delicious layer of fruit filling made up of this superfruit trio (which totally makes it healthy, right?).

4 cups (540 g) frozen mixed berries

2 tablespoons (30 ml) cornstarch

½ cup (100 g) granulated white sugar

2 cups (320 g) White Cake Mix (page 20)

½ cup or 1 stick (4 ounces/113 g) unsalted butter, sliced into ¼-inch-thick (6 mm) squares

1 Preheat oven to 350°F (175°C). Grease or line a 9 × 13-inch (23 × 33 cm) baking pan.

2 Dump and evenly spread berries in pan. Sprinkle berries with cornstarch, then sugar.

3 Evenly sprinkle dry cake mix across pan. Spread butter slices evenly across top.

4 Bake for 45–50 minutes. About 30 minutes in, quickly check the cake. Use a spatula or large wooden spoon to push down any uncooked cake mix into the bubbling mixture. Do not worry if this breaks the surface of the cake. Let the cake continue to bake for an additional 15–20 minutes, until the surface is completely golden brown.

5 Let cake cool for about 30 minutes before serving as the fruit layer will be extremely hot. If desired, serve with a scoop of your favorite ice cream and/or any of the toppings provided on pages 168–173.

STRAWBERRY JELL-O COBBLER

Prep time: 10–15 minutes   Cook time: 30–35 minutes

Serves 9–12

This is such a fun cake. Not only is there a layer of strawberry pie–like filling, but there's strawberry Jell-O mixed into the strawberry filling! It's a great way to get your kids to eat fruit without them even knowing it.

2 cups (300 g) frozen hulled strawberries

¼ cup (60 g) strawberry Jell-O crystals

1 cup (160 g) White Cake Mix (page 20)

¼ cup or ½ stick (2 ounces/57 g) unsalted butter, sliced into ¼-inch-thick (6 mm) squares

1   Preheat oven to 350°F (175°C). Grease or line a 9 × 9-inch (23 × 23 cm) baking pan.

2   Dump and spread strawberries evenly across bottom of pan. Sprinkle strawberries with Jell-O crystals. Evenly sprinkle cake mix in pan. Spread butter slices evenly across top.

3   Bake for about 30–35 minutes. About 25 minutes in, quickly check the cake. Use a spatula or large spoon to push down any uncooked cake mix into the bubbling mixture. Do not worry if this breaks the surface of the cake. Let the cake continue to bake for an additional 5–10 minutes, until the surface is golden brown.

4   Let cake cool for about 20 minutes before serving. If desired, serve with a scoop of your favorite ice cream and/or any of the toppings provided on pages 168–173.

SWEET PUMPKIN CAKE

Prep time: 10–15 minutes   Cook time: 35–40 minutes

Serves 9–12

Think mashed sweet potatoes, but with sweetened pumpkin purée—and topped with a buttery cake-mix crust. This cake is the ultimate in comfort food. I could eat the entire pan myself!

1 cup (225 g) canned pumpkin purée

½ cup (100 g) granulated white sugar

½ cup (80 g) Spice Cake Mix (page 19)

¼ cup or ½ stick (2 ounces/57 g) unsalted butter, sliced into ¼-inch-thick (6 mm) squares

1 Preheat oven to 350°F (175°C). Grease or line a 9 × 9-inch (23 × 23 cm) baking pan.

2 Evenly spread pumpkin purée across bottom of pan. Sprinkle with sugar.

3 Evenly sprinkle dry cake mix across pan. Spread butter slices evenly across top.

4 Bake for 35–40 minutes. About 25 minutes in, quickly check the cake. Use a spatula or large spoon to push down any uncooked cake mix into the bubbling mixture. Do not worry if this breaks the surface of the cake. Let the cake continue to bake for an additional 10–15 minutes, until the surface is dark golden brown.

5 Let cake cool for about 20–30 minutes before serving as the fruit layer will be extremely hot. If desired, serve with a scoop of your favorite ice cream and/or any of the toppings provided on pages 168–173.

PINEAPPLE UPSIDE-DOWN CAKE

Prep time: 20–25 minutes   Cook time: 40–45 minutes

Serves 9–12

I've always loved the idea of a pineapple upside-down cake. Normally, the bottom side of a cake is the ugly side that no one wants to see. The pineapple upside-down cake is one of the few exceptions to the rule, where, once flipped over, you're greeted by the sight of beautiful pineapple rings with cherries.

6 fresh peeled pineapple rings, sliced to ½-inch (13 mm) thickness

6 maraschino cherry halves

1½ teaspoons (7.5 ml) cornstarch

¼ cup (50 g) granulated white sugar

2 cups (320 g) White Cake Mix (page 20)

½ cup or 1 stick (4 ounces/113 g) unsalted butter, sliced into ¼-inch-thick (6 mm) squares

1 Preheat oven to 350°F (175°C). Line a 9 × 13-inch (23 × 33 cm) baking pan with parchment paper, making sure to leave enough overhang so that you can later lift the parchment paper with the cake in it.

2 Place pineapple rings, side by side, across the bottom of the pan. Place one cherry half in the center of each ring.

3 Sprinkle pineapples with cornstarch, then sugar. Sprinkle dry cake mix evenly across pan. Spread butter slices evenly across top.

4 Bake for 40–45 minutes. About 30 minutes in, quickly check the cake. Use a spatula or large spoon to push down any uncooked cake mix into the bubbling mixture. Do not worry if this breaks the surface of the cake. Let the cake continue to bake for an additional 10–15 minutes, until the surface is completely golden brown.

5 Let cake cool for about 30 minutes before serving as the fruit layer will be extremely hot. Carefully lift parchment paper and flip cake over so that the bottom becomes the top. Cut and serve. If desired, serve with a scoop of your favorite ice cream and/or any of the toppings provided on pages 168–173.

See page 22 for recipe photo.

CHOCOHOLIC DUMP CAKES

—— • ——

I'm a chocolate addict. I can't get through the day without at least one piece of chocolate. Have you ever heard the saying "a chocolate a day keeps the doctor away"? No? Well, it should be a saying. In my opinion, no dessert cookbook is complete without a section devoted to chocolate.

One of the things you'll notice in this chapter is that some of the recipes don't follow the classic dump cake rule of fruit on the bottom. When I started this journey, I didn't want to just include fruit with cake mix recipes. I was determined to make a dump cake without that fruit layer at the bottom. After much experimentation, I finally was able to achieve what I was looking for. Like your traditional dump cakes, the cake layer is thin. If it were thick, it simply couldn't cook without pre-mixing all the ingredients together. But these thin cake bars, brownies, and even cookies are still delicious.

BLUEBERRY CHOCOLATE CHEESECAKE

Prep time: 10–15 minutes   Cook time: 30–35 minutes

Serves 9–12

What's better than classic cheesecake? Flavored cheesecake! I love flavored cheesecakes, especially chocolate ones. Whenever I visit a cheesecake bakery, I end up choosing about half a dozen different cheesecake slices and at least one of them is always a chocolate-flavored one. This dessert combines thick blueberry sauce, sweetened cream cheese, and chocolate cake for a chocoholic twist on the original.

2 cups (300 g) fresh blueberries

1 tablespoon (15 ml) cornstarch

½ cup (100 g) granulated white sugar, divided

4 ounces (115 g) cream cheese, cut into ½-inch (13 mm) cubes

1 cup (155 g) Chocolate Cake Mix (page 18)

¼ cup or ½ stick (2 ounces/57 g) unsalted butter, sliced into ¼-inch-thick (6 mm) squares

1. Preheat oven to 350°F (175°C). Grease or line a 9 × 9-inch (23 × 23 cm) baking pan.

2. Dump and evenly spread blueberries across bottom of pan. Sprinkle berries with cornstarch, then with ¼ cup (50 g) sugar.

3. Place cream cheese cubes evenly across pan and sprinkle with remaining ¼ cup sugar. Sprinkle dry cake mix evenly across mixture. Spread butter slices evenly across top.

4. Bake for 30–35 minutes. About 25 minutes in, quickly check the cake. Use a spatula or large wooden spoon to push down any uncooked cake mix into the bubbling mixture. Do not worry if this breaks the surface of the cake. Let the cake continue to bake for approximately 5-10 minutes more, until cake mix looks completely cooked.

5. Let cake cool for about 20–30 minutes before serving as the fruit layer will be extremely hot. If desired, serve with a scoop of your favorite ice cream and/or any of the toppings provided on pages 168–173.

CHOCOLATE-COVERED STRAWBERRIES CAKE

Prep time: 10–15 minutes   Cook time: 35–40 minutes

Serves 9–12

What is it about chocolate-covered strawberries that gets us all giddy with excitement, makes us automatically exclaim "ooh," and leaves us unable to resist eating at least one? I'm asking because I don't know the answer. What I do know is that I love them, and while this cake doesn't look quite as lovely as a fresh strawberry dipped in chocolate, it does taste deliciously of strawberries and chocolate in cake form.

2 cups (300 g) frozen hulled strawberries

1 tablespoon (15 ml) cornstarch

½ cup (100 g) granulated white sugar

1 cup (175 g) semisweet or bittersweet chocolate chips

1 cup (155 g) Chocolate Cake Mix (page 18)

¼ cup or ½ stick (2 ounces/57 g) unsalted butter, sliced into ¼-inch-thick (6 mm) squares

1 Preheat oven to 350°F (175°C). Grease or line a 9 × 9-inch (23 × 23 cm) baking pan.

2 Dump and evenly spread strawberries across bottom of pan. Sprinkle strawberries evenly with cornstarch, then sugar. Scatter chocolate chips evenly across pan.

3 Sprinkle dry cake mix evenly across pan. Spread butter slices evenly across top.

4 Bake for 35–40 minutes. About 25 minutes in, quickly check the cake. Use a spatula or large wooden spoon to push down any uncooked cake mix into the bubbling mixture. Do not worry if this breaks the surface of the cake. Let the cake continue to bake for an additional 10–15 minutes, until cake mix looks completely cooked.

5 Let cake cool for about 20 minutes before serving as the fruit layer will be extremely hot. If desired, serve with a scoop of your favorite ice cream and/or any of the toppings provided on pages 168–173.

CHOCOLATE CHERRY CRISP

— • ◦ • —

Prep time: 10–15 minutes   Cook time: 40–45 minutes

Serves 9–12

You don't often find recipes for chocolate-flavored fruit crisps. In fact, I had never even eaten one until I made one myself. And I only wish I had thought to do it sooner! It's the perfect solution for chocoholics who find regular fruit crisps to be "too fruity" and in need of some chocolate. This chocolate cherry crisp consists of juicy cherries and a thin layer of chocolate and oat topping.

2½ cups (275 g) frozen pitted cherries

2 tablespoons (60 ml) cornstarch

½ cup (100 g) granulated white sugar

½ cup (78 g) Chocolate Cake Mix (page 18)

½ cup (40 g) quick oats

¼ cup or ½ stick (2 ounces/57 g) butter, sliced into ¼-inch-thick (6 mm) squares

1   Preheat oven to 350°F (175°C). Grease or line a 9 × 9-inch (23 × 23 cm) baking pan.

2   Dump and evenly spread cherries across bottom of pan. Evenly sprinkle cherries with cornstarch, then sugar.

3   Sprinkle dry cake mix evenly across pan. Scatter oats across cake mix. Spread butter slices evenly across top.

4   Bake for 40–45 minutes. About 25 minutes in, quickly check the cake. Use a spatula or large wooden spoon to push down any uncooked cake mix into the bubbling mixture. Do not worry if this breaks the surface of the cake. Let the cake continue to bake for an additional 15–20 minutes, until cake mix looks completely cooked.

5   Let cake cool for about 20 minutes before serving as the fruit layer will be extremely hot. If desired, serve with a scoop of your favorite ice cream and/or any of the toppings provided on pages 168–173.

CHOCOLATE COOKIE BARS

Prep time: 10–15 minutes   Cook time: 20–25 minutes

Serves 9–12

These crunchy chocolate cookie bars are such a sweet and fun treat for kids and adults alike. No need to get your hands dirty with dough balls—just add all ingredients to the pan, bake, and cut into squares.

3 tablespoons (1½ ounces/43 g) unsalted butter, melted, divided

1 cup (155 g) Chocolate Cake Mix (page 18), sifted (see page 15)

¼ cup (45 g) semisweet chocolate chips

3 tablespoons (45 ml) lemon-lime soda (or the homemade version on page 173)

1   Preheat oven to 325ºF (170ºC). Grease or line a 9 × 9-inch (23 × 23 cm) baking pan.

2   Evenly spread 2 tablespoons (30 ml) melted butter across bottom of pan. Shift pan around, as needed, to make sure butter coats the entire bottom. Sift in dry cake mix. Sprinkle with chocolate chips. Drizzle soda and remaining 1 tablespoon (15 ml) butter evenly over cake mix.

3   Bake for about 20–25 minutes. About 15 minutes in, quickly check the cake. Use a spatula or large spoon to push down any uncooked cake mix into the bubbling mixture. Do not worry if this breaks the surface of the cake. Let the cake continue to bake for an additional 5–10 minutes, until cake mix is completely cooked.

4   Let cake cool for about 20 minutes before cutting and serving.

GOOEY CARAMEL CHOCOLATE CAKE

———— • • • ————

Prep time: 10–15 minutes   Cook time: 30–35 minutes
Serves 9–12

Warm, gooey, and with melted chocolate morsels in every bite, this cake is sure to satisfy the most intense chocolate craving. What's not to love? Get a spoon and dig right in, or serve in bowls and top with ice cream if you feel like sharing!

¼ cup (60 ml) lemon-lime soda (or the homemade version on page 173)

¼ cup (60 ml) thick caramel sauce (you may need to warm your jar for easy pouring)

1 cup (155 g) Chocolate Cake Mix (page 18), sifted (see page 15)

¼ cup (60 ml) sweetened condensed milk

¼ cup (45 g) semisweet chocolate chips

¼ cup or ½ stick (2 ounces/57 g) unsalted butter, sliced into ¼-inch-thick (6 mm) squares

1 Preheat oven to 350°F (175°C). Grease or line a 9 × 9-inch (23 × 23 cm) baking pan. If lining baking pan, make sure to also grease it (see page 14).

2 Pour soda across bottom of pan. Drizzle caramel sauce evenly across pan.

3 Sift dry cake mix evenly across pan. Drizzle condensed milk across cake mix. Scatter with chocolate chips. Spread butter slices evenly across top.

4 Bake for 30–35 minutes. About 25 minutes in, quickly check the cake. Use a spatula or large spoon to moisten any uncooked cake mix, by spreading from wet sections next to it. Do not worry if this breaks the surface of the cake. Let the cake continue to bake for an additional 5–10 minutes, until all cake mix looks cooked.

5 Let cake cool for about 20 minutes before serving. If desired, serve with a scoop of your favorite ice cream and/or any of the toppings provided on pages 168–173.

CHOCOLATE STOUT CAKE

Prep time: 15–20 minutes   Cook time: 35–40 minutes

Serves 9–12

With its hint of coffee, stout beer brings chocolate cake to a whole new level. The bitter notes keep this cake from being overly rich and sweet, which makes it perfect if you're looking for something a little less chocolatey.

1 cup (155 g) Chocolate Cake Mix (page 18), sifted (see page 15)

¾ cup (175 ml) stout beer

¼ cup (50 g) granulated white sugar

½ cup (90 g) semisweet or bittersweet chocolate chips

¼ cup or ½ stick (2 ounces/57 g) unsalted butter, melted

1   Preheat oven to 350°F (175°C). Grease or line a 9 × 9-inch (23 × 23 cm) baking pan. If lining baking pan, make sure to also grease the surface of the parchment paper after lining it (see page 14).

2   Sift dry cake mix evenly across pan. Slowly pour beer over cake mix, trying to saturate as much of the cake mix as possible; then sprinkle evenly with sugar. Scatter chocolate chips across cake mix. Pour melted butter evenly across top, trying to saturate any cake mix that still remains dry.

3   Bake for 35–40 minutes. About 25 minutes in, quickly check the cake. Use a spatula or large spoon to moisten any uncooked cake mix, by spreading from the wet sections next to it. Do not worry if this breaks the surface of the cake. Let the cake continue to bake for an additional 10–15 minutes, until all cake mix looks cooked.

4   Let cake cool for about 20 minutes to allow it to set before cutting and serving. If desired, serve with a scoop of your favorite ice cream and/or any of the toppings provided on pages 168–173.

COCOA BERRY CRUMBLE

Prep time: 10–15 minutes   Cook time: 45–50 minutes

Serves 12–15

Here, the classic berry crumble is given a chocolate twist. Berries and chocolate make a delicious pairing—not to mention all the antioxidants in both! If you love berry crumbles and you love chocolate, you'll love this dessert with its chocolate-flavored buttery crust.

4 cups (540 g) frozen mixed berries

2 tablespoons (30 ml) cornstarch

½ cup (100 g) granulated white sugar

2 cups (310 g) Chocolate Cake Mix (page 18)

½ cup or 1 stick (4 ounces/113 g) unsalted butter, sliced into ¼-inch-thick (6 mm) squares

1   Preheat oven to 350°F (175°C). Grease or line a 9 × 13-inch (23 × 33 cm) baking pan.

2   Dump and evenly spread berries in pan. Sprinkle berries evenly with cornstarch, then sugar.

3   Evenly sprinkle dry cake mix across pan. Spread butter slices evenly across top.

4   Bake for 45–50 minutes. About 30 minutes in, quickly check the cake. Use a spatula or large spoon to push down any uncooked cake mix into the bubbling mixture. Do not worry if this breaks the surface of the cake. Let the cake continue to bake for an additional 15–20 minutes, until the cake mix looks completely cooked.

5   Let cake cool for about 30 minutes before serving as the fruit layer will be extremely hot. If desired, serve with a scoop of your favorite ice cream and/or any of the toppings provided on pages 168–173.

CHOCOLATE CHIP COOKIE BARS

Prep time: 10–15 minutes   Cook time: 30–35 minutes

Serves 9–12

This recipe makes a large sheet of chocolate chip–studded cookie cake, perfect for serving at a kids' party.

1 cup (235 ml) vanilla ice cream, melted

1 cup (160 g) White Cake Mix (page 20), sifted (see page 15)

½ cup (90 g) semisweet chocolate chips

¼ cup or ½ stick (2 ounces/57 g) unsalted butter, sliced into ¼-inch-thick (6 mm) squares

1   Preheat oven to 350°F (175°C). Grease or line a 9 × 9-inch (23 × 23 cm) baking pan.

2   Pour melted ice cream across bottom of dish. Evenly sift in dry cake mix. Sprinkle chocolate chips across cake mix. Spread butter slices evenly across top.

3   Bake for approximately 30–35 minutes. About 20 minutes in, quickly check the cake. Use a spatula or large spoon to moisten any uncooked cake mix by spreading from any wet sections next to it. Do not worry if this breaks the surface of the cake. Let the cake continue to bake for an additional 10–15 minutes, until the surface is golden brown.

4   Let cake cool for about 15–20 minutes before cutting and serving.

CHOCOLATE-PEANUT BUTTER CUP CAKE

— • • • —

Prep time: 10–15 minutes   Cook time: 20–25 minutes

Serves 9–12

This chocolate cake has a crunchy, chewy texture thanks to the peanut butter cups, which melt into the cake while baking. This dessert is sure to be a hit among the peanut butter and chocolate lovers in your life!

1 cup (235 ml) chocolate ice cream, melted

1 cup (140 g) chopped peanut butter candy cups

1 cup (155 g) Chocolate Cake Mix (page 18), sifted (see page 15)

¼ cup or ½ stick (2 ounces/57 g) unsalted butter, melted

1   Preheat oven to 350°F (175°C). Grease or line a 9 × 9-inch (23 × 23 cm) baking pan.

2   Pour melted ice cream across bottom of pan. Scatter peanut butter cup pieces. Sift in cake mix. Drizzle cake mix evenly with butter.

3   Bake for about 20–25 minutes. About 15 minutes in, quickly check the cake. Use a spatula or large spoon to moisten any uncooked cake mix by spreading from any wet sections next to it. Do not worry if this breaks the surface of the cake. Let the cake continue to bake for an additional 5–10 minutes, until all cake mix looks cooked.

4   Let cake cool for about 20 minutes before serving. If desired, serve with a scoop of your favorite ice cream and/or any of the toppings provided on pages 168–173.

PEANUT BUTTER CHOCOLATE CAKE

———— ◆•◆ ————

Prep time: 10–15 minutes   Cook time: 30–35 minutes

Serves 9–12

This cake contains dollops of peanut butter throughout for a delicious peanut buttery surprise. The peanut butter keeps the cake moist and chewy and adds a wonderful richness to this dessert, especially if you love peanut butter!

¼ cup (60 ml) lemon-lime soda (or the homemade version on page 173)

1 cup (155 g) Chocolate Cake Mix (page 18), sifted (see page 15)

½ cup (130 g) peanut butter

¼ cup or ½ stick (2 ounces/57 g) unsalted butter, sliced into ¼-inch-thick (6 mm) squares

1 Preheat oven to 350°F (175°C). Grease or line a 9 × 9-inch (23 × 23 cm) baking pan. If lining baking pan, make sure to also grease the surface of the parchment paper after lining it (see page 14).

2 Pour soda across bottom of pan.

3 Evenly sift dry cake mix across pan. In 1 teaspoon dollops, place peanut butter evenly across cake mix. Spread butter slices evenly across top.

4 Bake for 30–35 minutes. About 25 minutes in, quickly check the cake. Use a spatula or large spoon to moisten any uncooked cake mix, by spreading from wet sections next to it. Do not worry if this breaks the surface of the cake. Let the cake continue to bake for an additional 5–10 minutes, until all cake mix looks cooked. It is okay to remove the cake from the oven even if it is still bubbling.

5 Let cake cool for about 20 minutes before serving. If desired, serve with a scoop of your favorite ice cream and/or any of the toppings provided on pages 168–173.

FUDGY BROWNIES

Prep time: 10–15 minutes   Cook time: 30–35 minutes

Serves 9–12

Remember at the start of this chapter when I discussed making dump cakes without that fruit bottom layer? Well, here is the first such recipe!

These brownies may not bake up as thick as traditional brownies, but they are just as rich and packed with chocolate bliss. The chocolate syrup (you can use the homemade version or store-bought) makes the brownies extra fudgy.

¼ cup (60 ml) lemon-lime soda (or the homemade version on page 173)

½ cup (120 ml) chocolate syrup, divided (your favorite brand or the homemade version on page 169)

1 cup (155 g) Chocolate Cake Mix (page 18), sifted (see page 15)

¼ cup or ½ stick (2 ounces/57 g) unsalted butter, sliced into ¼-inch-thick (6 mm) squares

1. Preheat oven to 350°F (175°C). Grease or line a 9 × 13-inch (23 × 33 cm) baking pan. If lining baking pan, make sure to also grease it (see page 14).

2. Pour soda across bottom of pan. Drizzle in ¼ cup (60 ml) chocolate syrup evenly across pan.

3. Sift dry cake mix evenly across pan. Drizzle remaining ¼ cup (60 ml) chocolate syrup evenly across cake mix. Spread butter slices evenly across top.

4. Bake for 30–35 minutes. About 25 minutes in, quickly check the cake. Use a spatula or large spoon to moisten any uncooked cake mix, by spreading from wet sections next to it. Do not worry if this breaks the surface of the cake. Let the cake continue to bake for an additional 5–10 minutes, until all cake mix looks cooked.

5. Let cake cool for about 20 minutes to allow it to set before cutting and serving.

CHOCOLATE BANANA CAKE

Prep time: 10–15 minutes   Cook time: 30–35 minutes

Serves 9–12

It's one of life's greatest decisions: regular banana bread or chocolate banana bread? Maybe I'm exaggerating a little bit, but it's definitely a dilemma I have when trying to decide what to do with those pesky brown bananas. I often end up making both because I simply can't decide. And even when I'm eating them both side by side, I still can't decide which one I prefer! That's why I've included this recipe for a chocolate version of my simplified banana cake (page 28).

2 very ripe medium bananas, peeled and cut into ¼-inch-thick (6 mm) slices

¼ cup (60 g) light brown sugar, packed

1 teaspoon (5 ml) ground cinnamon

1 cup (155 g) Chocolate Cake Mix (page 18)

¼ cup or ½ stick (2 ounces/57 g) unsalted butter, sliced into ¼-inch-thick (6 mm) squares

1   Preheat oven to 350°F (175°C). Grease or line a 9 × 9-inch (23 × 23 cm) baking pan.

2   Dump and spread banana slices evenly across bottom of pan. You should have enough to line the entire bottom layer, with the slices side by side and touching, and then enough left over for a more spread-out layer on top.

3   Sprinkle brown sugar evenly across bananas. Then, sprinkle dry cake mix evenly across bananas. Spread butter slices evenly across top.

4   Bake for 30–35 minutes. About 20 minutes in, quickly check the cake. Use a spatula or large spoon to push down any uncooked cake mix into the bubbling mixture. Do not worry if this breaks the surface of the cake. Let the cake continue to bake for an additional 10–15 minutes, until the surface is completely golden brown.

5   Let cake cool for about 20–30 minutes before serving as the fruit layer will be extremely hot. If desired, serve with a scoop of your favorite ice cream and/or any of the toppings provided on pages 168–173.

SINGLE-SERVING DUMP CAKES

There are days when you just need one single-serving dessert (basically at the end of every day). If you're just baking for yourself, you likely don't want to have an entire cake. Or if you are like me and lack the self-control to stop at one piece when there's a full cake in front of you, then these single-serving cakes are the solution.

APPLE SPICE COBBLER

Prep time: 10–15 minutes Cook time: 35–40 minutes

Serves 1

Warm apple cinnamon cake topped with vanilla ice cream. Is there a better way to end your night? You'll be having sweet dreams after eating this dessert.

½ cup (75 g) peeled fresh apple cubes, approximately ½-inch (13 mm) cubes

1 teaspoon (5 ml) cornstarch

1 tablespoon (15 ml) granulated white sugar

¼ cup (40 g) Spice Cake Mix (page 19)

1 tablespoon (½ ounce/14 g) unsalted butter, melted

1 Preheat oven to 350°F (175°C). Grease an 8-ounce (235 ml) round ramekin or similarly sized baking dish that measures 4 inches in diameter.

2 Spread apple cubes evenly across bottom of baking dish. Sprinkle with cornstarch, then sugar.

3 Sprinkle dry cake mix evenly across ramekin. Starting at the center of the dish, pour melted butter over top.

4 Bake for 35–40 minutes. About 25 minutes in, quickly check the cake. Use a spatula or large wooden spoon to push down any uncooked cake mix into the bubbling mixture. Do not worry if this breaks the surface of the cake. Let the cake continue to bake for an additional 10–15 minutes, until the surface is golden brown.

5 Let cake cool for about 20 minutes before serving as the fruit layer will be extremely hot. If desired, serve with a scoop of your favorite ice cream and/or any of the toppings provided on pages 168–173.

MIXED BERRY CRISP

— ◆ ● ◆ —

Prep time: 10–15 minutes   Cook time: 30–35 minutes
Serves 1

Can't choose a favorite berry? This dessert contains several! Can't decide between a buttery crumble or a crunchy oat crisp? This cake has both! It's the ultimate dessert for the indecisive.

¼ cup (34 g) frozen mixed berries of your choice

½ teaspoon (2.5 ml) cornstarch

1 tablespoon (15 ml) granulated white sugar

2 tablespoons (30 ml) white cake mix (page 20)

2 tablespoons (30 ml) quick oats

1 tablespoon (½ ounce/14 g) unsalted butter, melted

1   Preheat oven to 350°F (175°C). Grease an 8-ounce (235 ml) round ramekin that measures 4 inches (10 cm) in diameter.

2   Dump berries into ramekin. Sprinkle with cornstarch, then sugar.

3   Sprinkle dry cake mix, then quick oats evenly across ramekin. Starting in the center of the dish, pour melted butter over top.

4   Bake for 30–35 minutes. About 25 minutes in, quickly check the cake. Use a spatula or large wooden spoon to push down any uncooked cake mix into the bubbling mixture. Do not worry if this breaks the surface of the cake. Let the cake continue to bake for an additional 5–10 minutes, until the cake mix looks completely cooked.

5   Let cake cool for about 20 minutes before serving as the fruit layer will be extremely hot. If desired, serve with a scoop of your favorite ice cream.

JUST CHOCOLATE CAKE

• ● ●

Prep time: 10–15 minutes   Cook time: 25 minutes

Serves 1

Some days I just want a plain chocolate cake. No nuts, no added fruits. Just pure chocolate bliss.

2 tablespoons (1 ounce/28 g) unsalted butter, melted

¾ cup (116 g) Chocolate Cake Mix (page 18), sifted (see page 15)

¼ cup (45 g) semisweet chocolate chips

2 tablespoons (30 ml) unsalted butter, thinly sliced

1   Preheat oven to 350°F (175°C). Grease a small round baking dish that measures about 5½ inches (14 cm) in diameter.

2   Pour melted butter across bottom of dish. Sift in cake mix.

3   Scatter chocolate chips over cake mix. Spread butter slices evenly across top.

4   Bake for approximately 25 minutes. About 20 minutes in, quickly check the cake. Use a spatula or large spoon to moisten any uncooked cake mix, by spreading from wet sections next to it. Do not worry if this breaks the surface of the cake. Let the cake continue to bake for an additional 5 minutes, until cake mix is completely cooked.

5   Let cake cool for about 10 minutes before digging in. If desired, serve with a scoop of your favorite ice cream and/or any of the toppings provided on pages 168–173.

COOKIES AND CREAM COOKIE CAKE

Prep time: 10–15 minutes   Cook time: 25–30 minutes

Serves 1

It's a cookie within a cookie! This extra-large cookie cake is studded with crushed Oreo cookies for double the cookie pleasure. Eat it all by yourself or split it with a loved one!

½ cup (120 ml) full-fat vanilla ice cream, melted

½ cup (80 g) White Cake Mix (page 20), sifted (see page 15)

2 Oreo cookies, crushed by hand into small pieces

2 tablespoons (1 ounce/28 g) unsalted butter, melted

1   Preheat oven to 350°F (175°C). Grease a small round baking dish that measures 5 to 5½ inches (12.7 cm to 14 cm) in diameter and at least 2 inches (5 cm) tall.

2   Pour melted ice cream into bottom of dish. Sift in cake mix.

3   Scatter crushed Oreos over cake mix. Starting at the center, pour melted butter across top.

4   Bake for approximately 25–30 minutes. About 20 minutes in, quickly check the cake. Use a spatula or large spoon to moisten any uncooked cake mix, by spreading from wet sections next to it. Do not worry if this breaks the surface of the cake. Let the cake continue to bake for an additional 5–10 minutes, until the surface is golden brown.

5   Let cake cool for about 10 minutes before digging in. If desired, serve with a scoop of your favorite ice cream and/or any of the toppings provided on pages 168–173.

CHERRY CHOCOLATE CHIP COBBLER

Prep time: 10–15 minutes   Cook time: 30–35 minutes

Serves 1

Growing up, one of my favorite ice cream flavors was cherry chocolate chip, with its lovely pink hue and chocolate chunks mixed right in. This sweet treat combines both flavors, for a cherry chocolate-chip cobbler.

½ cup (78 g) frozen pitted cherries

1 teaspoon (5 ml) cornstarch

1 tablespoon (15 ml) granulated white sugar

¼ cup (40 g) Chocolate Cake Mix (page 18)

2 tablespoons (30 ml) semisweet or bittersweet chocolate chips

1 tablespoon (½ ounce/14 g) unsalted butter, melted

1   Preheat oven to 350°F (175°C). Grease an 8-ounce (235 ml) round ramekin or similarly sized baking dish that measures 4 inches (10 cm) in diameter and is at least 2 inches (5 cm) tall.

2   Dump cherries into bottom of baking dish. Sprinkle with cornstarch, then sugar.

3   Sprinkle dry cake mix evenly across ramekin. Top with chocolate chips. Starting at the center of the dish, pour melted butter across top.

4   Bake for 30–35 minutes. About 25 minutes in, quickly check the cake. Use a spatula or large wooden spoon to push down any uncooked cake mix into the bubbling mixture. Do not worry if this breaks the surface of the cake. Let the cake continue to bake for an additional 5–10 minutes, until the cake mix looks completely cooked.

5   Let cake cool for about 20 minutes before serving as the fruit layer will be extremely hot. If desired, serve with a scoop of your favorite ice cream and/or any of the toppings provided on pages 168–173.

BIRTHDAY COOKIE CAKE

—— •–•–• ——

Prep time: 10–15 minutes   Cook time: 25–30 minutes
Serves 1

This cookie cake is crunchy and chewy in all the right places. It's baked in a round baking dish, making it almost like a deep-dish cookie! The sprinkles in the Funfetti Cake Mix make it really seem like a birthday cake in cookie form.

½ cup (125 ml) full-fat vanilla ice cream, melted

½ cup (80 g) Funfetti Cake Mix (page 19), sifted (see page 15)

2 tablespoons or ¼ stick (1 ounce/28 g) unsalted butter, melted

1   Preheat oven to 350°F (175°C). Grease a small round baking dish that measures 5 to 5½ inches (12.7 cm to 14 cm) in diameter and at least 2 inches (5 cm) tall.

2   Pour melted ice cream across bottom of dish. Sift cake mix evenly over ice cream.

3   Starting at the center of the dish, evenly pour in the melted butter.

4   Bake for approximately 25–30 minutes. About 20 minutes in, quickly check the cake. Use a spatula or large spoon to moisten any uncooked cake mix, spreading from wet sections next to it. Do not worry if this breaks the surface of the cake. Let the cake continue to bake for an additional 5–10 minutes, until the surface is golden brown.

5   Let cake cool for about 10 minutes before digging in. If desired, serve with a scoop of your favorite ice cream and/or any of the toppings provided on pages 168–173.

COCONUT RUM CAKE

- - - ◆ ● ◆ - - -

Prep time: 10–15 minutes   Cook time: 30–35 minutes

Serves 1

Sweet coconut flakes and just a touch of rum make a sweet, fluffy, and gooey cake just for one. It's a fun little happy hour treat you can enjoy after a long day at work.

2 tablespoons (30 ml) lemon-lime soda (or the homemade version on page 173)

¼ cup (40 g) White Cake Mix (page 20)

2 tablespoons (30 ml) dark rum

¼ cup (23 g) sweetened coconut flakes

1 tablespoon (½ ounce/14 g) unsalted butter, melted

1   Preheat oven to 350°F (175°C). Grease an 8-ounce (235 ml) round ramekin or other similarly sized round baking dish that measures 4 inches (10 cm) in diameter and is at least 2 inches (5 cm) tall.

2   Pour soda into bottom of baking dish. Sprinkle dry cake mix evenly across top. Drizzle cake mix with rum. Evenly sprinkle the coconut flakes on top, covering the entire surface. Starting at the center, pour melted butter across top.

3   Bake for 30–35 minutes, until the surface of the cake is golden brown.

4   Let cake cool for about 10 minutes before digging in. If desired, serve with a scoop of your favorite ice cream and/or any of the toppings provided on pages 168–173.

CHOCOLATE BROWNIE

———— • • • ————

Prep time: 10–15 minutes   Cook time: 25–30 minutes

Serves 1

If there is one chocolate dessert I crave constantly, it's a brownie! There's something so unique about the rich chocolate flavor and dense and chewy texture that makes brownies so irresistible. This recipe makes just one single brownie, perfect for whenever the craving strikes.

1 tablespoon (15 ml) lemon-lime soda (or the homemade version on page 173)

¼ cup (40 g) Chocolate Cake Mix (page 18), sifted (see page 15)

2 tablespoons (30 ml) chocolate syrup (store-bought or the homemade version on page 169)

1 tablespoon (½ ounce/14 g) unsalted butter, melted

1   Preheat oven to 350°F (175°C). Grease an 8-ounce (235 ml) round ramekin or other similarly sized round baking dish that measures 4 inches (10 cm) in diameter and is at least 2 inches (5 cm) tall.

2   Pour soda into bottom of baking dish. Sift in dry cake mix. Drizzle chocolate syrup evenly across cake mix. Starting at the center of the dish, pour melted butter across top.

3   Bake for 25–30 minutes. About 15 minutes in, quickly check the cake. Use a spatula or large spoon to moisten any uncooked cake mix, by spreading from wet sections next to it. Do not worry if this breaks the surface of the cake. Let the cake continue to bake for an additional 10–15 minutes until all the cake mix looks cooked.

4   Let brownie cool for about 10 minutes before digging in. If desired, serve with a scoop of your favorite ice cream and/or any of the toppings provided on pages 168–173.

BERRYLICIOUS CRUMBLE

Prep time: 10–15 minutes   Cook time: 35–40 minutes

Serves 1

Your favorite berry crumble, now in single-serving size! Toss together a couple of ingredients and let the oven do the rest. You can also make multiple individual crumbles for an easy dinner party dessert that will impress your guests!

½ cup (70 g) frozen mixed berries

1 teaspoon (5 ml) cornstarch

1 tablespoon (15 ml) granulated white sugar

¼ cup (40 g) White Cake Mix (page 20)

1 tablespoon (½ ounce/14 g) unsalted butter, melted

1   Preheat oven to 350°F (175°C). Grease an 8-ounce (235 ml) round ramekin or similarly sized baking dish that measures 4 inches (10 cm) in diameter and is at least 2 inches (5 cm) tall.

2   Dump and spread berries evenly across bottom of baking dish. Sprinkle evenly with cornstarch, then sugar.

3   Sprinkle dry cake mix evenly across ramekin. Starting at the center of the dish, pour melted butter over top.

4   Bake for 35–40 minutes. About 25 minutes in, quickly check the cake. Use a spatula or large wooden spoon to push down any uncooked cake mix into the bubbling mixture. Do not worry if this breaks the surface of the cake. Let the cake continue to bake for an additional 10–15 minutes, until the surface is dark golden brown.

5   Let cake cool for about 20 minutes before serving as the fruit layer will be extremely hot. If desired, serve with a scoop of your favorite ice cream and/or any of the toppings provided on pages 168–173.

BLUEBERRY CLOUD CAKE

Prep time: 10–15 minutes   Cook time: 30–35 minutes

Serves 1

This delightful cake is a mix of fluffy, light angel food cake and fresh blueberries. The key to the incredibly delicate texture is angel food cake mix. While I've provided from-scratch versions for all the other cake mixes used in this book, this is the one exception. Angel food cake is made predominantly of egg whites and requires quite a lengthy preparation time. So for this recipe, we will be relying on the mix available at grocery stores.

Please note, this cake needs to be consumed right away. When it's first baked, it's almost soufflé-like. And much like a soufflé, it will sink once it cools and become somewhat gummy in texture. So please enjoy while warm!

¼ cup (38 g) fresh blueberries

¼ cup (30 g) store-bought angel food cake mix

¼ cup (60 ml) club soda

1   Preheat oven to 350°F (175°C). Grease an 8-ounce (235 ml) round ramekin or similarly sized baking dish that measures 4 inches (10 cm) in diameter and at least 2 inches (5 cm) tall.

2   Dump fresh berries into bottom of baking dish; they should cover almost the entire surface. Sprinkle dry cake mix evenly over blueberries.

3   Gently pour soda over surface of cake mix. The club soda should develop a thick foam. If there is any cake mix not covered by the foam, gently move it with a spatula until all cake mix is completely covered.

4   Bake for approximately 30–35 minutes. The top of the cake should be light golden brown and the edges should no longer look gooey. Let cake cool for a few moments before eating right away.

See page 6 for recipe photo.

GLUTEN-FREE DUMP CAKES

———— ◦ ◦ ◦ ————

I have many friends who are gluten intolerant, so I always try to have plenty of gluten-free recipes because no one should be denied dessert! With the help of gluten-free cake mix, almond flour, and quick oats, I've created several yummy gluten-free dump cakes. Some of them don't even require any cake mix!

BERRY OAT CRUMBLE

Prep time: 10–15 minutes   Cook time: 40 minutes
Serves 9–12

This is like the dessert version of oatmeal, with sweetened berries, crunchy oats, and toasted nuts. My version uses toasted pecans but feel free to substitute with walnuts, cashews, almonds, or any other nut!

2 cups (270 g) frozen mixed berries of your choice

1 tablespoon (15 ml) cornstarch

¼ cup (50 g) granulated white sugar

1 cup (80 g) gluten-free quick oats

¼ cup (60 g) light brown sugar, packed

1 cup (100 g) chopped pecans

¼ cup or ½ stick (2 ounces/57 g) butter, sliced into ¼-inch-thick (6 mm) squares

1   Preheat oven to 350°F (175°C). Grease or line a 9 × 9-inch (23 × 23 cm) baking pan.

2   Dump and evenly spread berries across bottom of pan. Sprinkle berries evenly with cornstarch, then sugar.

3   Sprinkle oats evenly across pan. Spread brown sugar over oats, and scatter with pecans. Spread butter slices evenly across top.

4   Bake for about 40 minutes. About 30 minutes in, quickly check the cake. Use a spatula or large wooden spoon to push down any uncooked cake mix into the bubbling mixture. Do not worry if this breaks the surface of the cake. Let the cake continue to bake for an additional 10 minutes, until the surface is dark golden brown.

5   Let cake cool for about 20 minutes before serving as the fruit layer will be extremely hot. If desired, serve with a scoop of your favorite ice cream and/or any of the toppings provided on pages 168–173.

BLUEBERRY CHOCOLATE COBBLER

Prep time: 10–15 minutes   Cook time: 35–40 minutes
Serves 9–12

This intensely chocolatey cobbler is mixed with deliciously sweet blueberries. It's almost like a blueberry brownie!

2 cups (310 g) frozen blueberries

1 tablespoon (15 ml) cornstarch

½ cup (100 g) granulated white sugar

1 cup (155 g) Gluten-Free Chocolate Cake Mix (page 21)

¼ cup or ½ cup (2 ounces/57 g) unsalted butter, sliced to ¼-inch-thick (6 mm) squares

1   Preheat oven to 350°F (175°C). Grease or line a 9 × 9-inch (23 × 23 cm) baking pan.

2   Dump and evenly spread blueberries across bottom of pan. Sprinkle blueberries evenly with cornstarch, then sugar.

3   Sprinkle dry cake mix evenly across pan. Spread butter slices evenly across top.

4   Bake for about 35–40 minutes. About 25 minutes in, quickly check the cake. Use a spatula or large wooden spoon to push down any uncooked cake mix into the bubbling mixture. Do not worry if this breaks the surface of the cake. Let the cake continue to bake for an additional 10–15 minutes, until the cake mix looks completely cooked.

5   Let cake cool for about 20 minutes before serving as the fruit layer will be extremely hot. If desired, serve with a scoop of your favorite ice cream and/or any of the toppings provided on pages 168–173.

PUMPKIN APPLE SPICE CAKE

Prep time: 10–15 minutes   Cook time: 35–40 minutes

Serves 9–12

Pumpkin purée is cooked with sweet apples for a delicious fall fruit combination that should keep you warm and snuggly as temperatures drop.

1 cup (225 g) canned pumpkin purée

1 teaspoon (5 ml) ground cinnamon

½ teaspoon (2.5 ml) ground nutmeg

½ cup (100 g) granulated white sugar

1 cup (150 g) cubed and peeled apples, in ½-inch (13 mm) cubes

½ cup (80 g) Gluten-Free White Cake Mix (page 20)

¼ cup or ½ stick (2 ounces/57 g) unsalted butter, sliced into ¼-inch-thick (6 mm) squares

1 Preheat oven to 350°F (175°C). Grease or line a 9 × 9-inch (23 × 23 cm) baking pan.

2 Evenly spread pumpkin purée across bottom of pan. Sprinkle pumpkin with cinnamon, then nutmeg, then sugar. Scatter apples across pumpkin.

3 Sprinkle dry cake mix evenly across pan. Spread butter slices evenly across top.

4 Bake for 35–40 minutes. About 25 minutes in, quickly check the cake. Use a spatula or large wooden spoon to push down any uncooked cake mix into the bubbling mixture. Do not worry if this breaks the surface of the cake. Let the cake continue to bake for an additional 10–15 minutes, until the surface is dark golden brown.

5 Let cake cool for about 20–30 minutes before serving as the fruit layer will be extremely hot. If desired, serve with a scoop of your favorite ice cream and/or any of the toppings provided on pages 168–173.

CHERRY CRUMBLE

- • ◆ • • -

Prep time: 10–15 minutes   Cook time: 40 minutes

Serves 9–12

My favorite fruit is the cherry, so you'll find quite a few cherry-flavored desserts in this book. I don't know what it is about them: their cute shape, the fact that they often come in pairs, or that audible crunch when you bite into them before the sweet juices hit. Whatever the reason, cherries are delicious and they are what make this crumble so great!

2 cups (310 g) frozen pitted cherries

1 tablespoon (15 ml) cornstarch

¼ cup (50 g) granulated white sugar

1 cup (160 g) Gluten-Free White Cake Mix (page 20)

1 cup (100 g) chopped pecans

¼ cup or ½ stick (2 ounces/57 g) unsalted butter, sliced to ¼-inch-thick (6 mm) squares

1 Preheat oven to 350°F (175°C). Grease or line a 9 × 9-inch (23 × 23 cm) baking pan.

2 Dump and evenly spread cherries across bottom of pan. Sprinkle cherries evenly with cornstarch, then sugar.

3 Sprinkle dry cake mix evenly across pan. Scatter with pecans. Spread butter slices evenly across top.

4 Bake for about 40 minutes. About 30 minutes in, quickly check the cake. Use a spatula or large wooden spoon to push down any uncooked cake mix into the bubbling mixture. Do not worry if this breaks the surface of the cake. Let the cake continue to bake for an additional 10 minutes, until the surface is dark golden brown.

5 Let cake cool for about 20 minutes before serving as the fruit layer will be extremely hot. If desired, serve with a scoop of your favorite ice cream and/or any of the toppings provided on pages 168–173.

MANGO DELIGHT CAKE

Prep time: 10–15 minutes   Cook time: 35–40 minutes

Serves 9–12

With sweet mangoes and toasted coconut, this cake makes me think I'm in Hawaii and always puts a smile on my face!

2 cups (350 g) frozen mango cubes

1 tablespoon (15 ml) cornstarch

½ cup (100 g) granulated white sugar

1 cup (160 g) Gluten-Free White Cake Mix (page 20)

½ cup (45 g) sweetened coconut flakes

¼ cup or ½ stick (2 ounces/57 g) unsalted butter, sliced into ¼-inch-thick (6 mm) squares

1 Preheat oven to 350°F (175°C). Grease or line a 9 × 9-inch (23 × 23 cm) baking pan.

2 Dump and evenly spread mangoes across bottom of pan. Sprinkle mangoes with cornstarch, then sugar. Sprinkle dry cake mix evenly across pan; then scatter mix with coconut flakes. Spread butter slices evenly across pan.

3 Bake for 35–40 minutes. About 25 minutes in, quickly check the cake. Use a spatula or large wooden spoon to push down any uncooked cake mix into the bubbling mixture. Do not worry if this breaks the surface of the cake. Let the cake continue to bake for an additional 10–15 minutes, until the surface is golden brown.

4 Let cake cool for about 20 minutes before serving as the fruit layer will be extremely hot. If desired, serve with a scoop of your favorite ice cream and/or any of the toppings provided on pages 168–173.

ALMOND CRUNCH CAKE

Prep time: 10–15 minutes   Cook time: 40–45 minutes

Serves 9–12

If you enjoy almonds, this cake gives you a double dose in the form of almond flour and chopped almonds, which add a delicious crunch to every bite.

2 cups (260 g) frozen
   blackberries

1 tablespoon (15 ml) cornstarch

½ cup (100 g) granulated
   white sugar

1 cup (125 g) almond flour

½ cup (63 g) chopped almonds

¼ cup or ½ stick (2 ounces/57 g)
   unsalted butter, sliced into
   ¼-inch-thick (6 mm) squares

1   Preheat oven to 350°F (175°C). Grease or line a 9 × 9-inch (23 × 23 cm) baking pan.

2   Dump and evenly spread berries across bottom of pan. Sprinkle with cornstarch, then sugar.

3   Sprinkle almond flour evenly across pan, then sprinkle almonds. Spread butter slices evenly across top.

4   Bake for about 40–45 minutes. About 30 minutes in, quickly check the cake. Use a spatula or large wooden spoon to push down any uncooked cake mix into the bubbling mixture. Do not worry if this breaks the surface of the cake. Let the cake continue to bake for an additional 10-15 minutes, until the surface is dark golden brown.

5   Let cake cool for about 20 minutes before serving as the fruit layer will be extremely hot. If desired, serve with a scoop of your favorite ice cream and/or any of the toppings provided on pages 168–173.

COCONUT MACAROON BARS

Prep time: 5–10 minutes   Cook time: 30–35 minutes

Serves 12–15

This cake tastes like chewy coconut macaroon cookies, but in sheet-cake form. With only two ingredients, it's ridiculously easy to make and comes out super tasty!

5 cups (450 g) sweetened coconut flakes

1 14-ounce (396 g) can sweetened condensed milk

1   Preheat oven to 350°F (175°C). Grease or line a 9 × 9-inch (23 × 23 cm) baking pan.

2   Dump and spread coconut evenly across pan. Drizzle sweetened condensed milk evenly over coconut, covering entire surface.

3   Bake for 30–35 minutes, or until surface is golden brown. Let cake fully cool (this may take an hour or two), before cutting into bars and serving.

MICROWAVE DUMP CAKES

— ◦ • ◦ —

While dump cakes are very easy to prepare, they do take almost as long to bake as traditional cakes. If you don't have the patience or just want something quick, try one of these microwave dump cakes. They aren't as photogenic as regular dump cakes because the cake layer stays pale and doesn't develop that golden-brown color you can only achieve through baking. However, they still taste delicious, especially if you're craving a late-night treat. Plus, they cook in less than 10 minutes! Make sure you don't leave out the soda in any of these microwave recipes. It's necessary to keep the cake mix from overcooking.

CHOCOLATE RASPBERRY CAKE

Prep time: 10 minutes   Cook time: 8–9 minutes

Serves 9–12

The lightness of the raspberries and denseness of the rich chocolate layer merge into one sweet and tart raspberry chocolate combination.

2 cups (250 g) fresh raspberries

1½ teaspoons (7.5 ml) cornstarch

½ cup (100 g) granulated white sugar

1 cup (155 g) Chocolate Cake Mix (page 18)

2 tablespoons (30 ml) lemon-lime soda (or the homemade version on page 173)

¼ cup or ½ stick (2 ounces/57 g) unsalted butter, sliced into ¼-inch-thick (6 mm) squares

1 Grease or line an 8 × 8-inch (20 × 20 cm) microwave-safe baking pan.

2 Dump and evenly spread raspberries across bottom of pan. Sprinkle berries with cornstarch, then sugar.

3 Sprinkle dry cake mix evenly across pan and drizzle with soda. Spread butter slices evenly across top.

4 Cover the top of your baking pan with a large sheet of parchment paper (large enough that it won't sink in). Microwave cake for approximately 7 minutes at full power. Remove parchment paper. Check the cake and use a spatula or large wooden spoon to push down any uncooked cake mix into the bubbling mixture. Cook uncovered for an additional 1–2 minutes, until cake mix is fully cooked. Be careful not to allow it to overcook, or the cake mix pieces will harden.

5 Cake should still be bubbling when finished. Let cool for about 20 minutes before eating.

MIXED BERRY MUG CRISP

Prep time: 5–10 minutes   Cook time: 2–3 minutes

Serves 1

This easy single-serving fruit crisp couldn't get any easier. It gives you the perfect excuse for eating a giant scoop of ice cream.

½ cup (68 g) frozen mixed berries of your choice

½ teaspoon (2.5 ml) cornstarch

1 tablespoon (15 ml) granulated white sugar

¼ cup (30 g) crunchy granola

1   Dump berries into an oversized, tall, microwave-safe mug. Sprinkle berries with cornstarch, then sugar. Pour granola across top.

2   Microwave cake, uncovered, at full power for 2–3 minutes, until berry juices have thickened.

3   Let cake cool for 10 minutes before eating. If desired, serve with a scoop of your favorite ice cream.

PEACHY CRUMBLE

Prep time: 10 minutes   Cook time: 11 minutes

Serves 9–12

Sometimes you need something warm, crunchy, and fruity. Oh, and you need it right now. With juicy sweet peaches and crunchy cake pieces, this easy microwave crumble is the answer.

1½ cups (375 g) frozen peach slices

1 tablespoon (15 ml) cornstarch

½ cup (100 g) granulated white sugar

1 cup (160 g) White Cake Mix (page 20)

¼ cup (60 ml) lemon-lime soda (or the homemade version on page 173)

¼ cup or ½ stick (2 ounces/57 g) unsalted butter, sliced into ¼-inch-thick (6 mm) squares

1   Grease or line an 8 × 8-inch (20 cm × 20 cm) microwave-safe glass baking pan.

2   Dump and evenly spread peaches across bottom of pan, making sure the slices are lying on their sides. Sprinkle peaches evenly with cornstarch, then sugar.

3   Sprinkle dry cake mix evenly across pan. Drizzle soda evenly across cake mix. Spread butter slices evenly across top.

4   Cover the top of your baking pan with a large sheet of parchment paper (large enough that it won't sink in). Microwave for approximately 8 minutes at full power until the juices from the peaches have thickened. Check the cake and use a spatula or large spoon to push down any uncooked cake mix into the bubbling mixture. Remove parchment paper and cook uncovered at full power for an additional 3 minutes. Be careful not to allow it to overcook, or the cake mix pieces will harden.

5   Remove from microwave and let cool about 20 minutes before eating.

COBBLER MUG CAKE

Prep time: 5–10 minutes   Cook time: 2 minutes

Serves 1

I wrote an entire book on mug cakes, so I couldn't resist coming up with a few mug dump cakes! A mug cake is a perfect single-serving dessert made in your favorite mug. It's a great excuse for buying that super cute mug you've been eyeing even though you already have an endless collection.

½ cup (68 g) frozen berries of your choice

½ teaspoon (2.5 ml) cornstarch

2 teaspoons (10 ml) granulated white sugar

¼ cup (40 g) White Cake Mix (page 20)

1 tablespoon (15 ml) soda

1 tablespoon (½ ounce/14 g) unsalted butter

1   Dump berries into an oversized, tall, microwave-safe mug. Sprinkle berries with cornstarch, then sugar. Sprinkle cake mix over berries. Your cobbler should only take up about half the mug, otherwise your ingredients may splatter out when cooking.

2   Pour soda over cake mix. Place butter in the center.

3   Microwave cake, uncovered, at full power for 1 minute. Check on cake and push any uncooked cake mix down into the berry mixture. Cook for an additional 1 minute at full power.

4   Let cake cool for 10 minutes before eating.

BLACKBERRY CRUMBLE

—— ◆ ——

Prep time: 10 minutes   Cook time: 5–7 minutes

Serves 9–12

Juicy blackberry-flavored pie-like filling, with buttery crumble mixed in. Don't worry that you can't see all the crumble; you'll find more pieces when you start digging in!

2 cups (260 g) frozen blackberries

1 tablespoon (15 ml) cornstarch

½ cup (100 g) granulated white sugar

½ cup (80 g) White Cake Mix (page 20)

2 tablespoons (30 ml) lemon-lime soda (or the homemade version on page 173)

¼ cup or ½ stick (2 ounces/57 g) unsalted butter, sliced into ¼-inch-thick (6 mm) squares

1   Grease or line an 8 × 8-inch (20 × 20 cm) microwave-safe glass baking pan.

2   Dump and evenly spread berries across bottom of pan. Sprinkle berries evenly with cornstarch, then sugar.

3   Sprinkle dry cake mix evenly across pan and drizzle with soda. Spread butter slices evenly across top.

4   Cover the top of your baking pan with a large sheet of parchment paper (large enough that it won't sink in). Microwave cake for approximately 4–5 minutes at full power. Remove parchment paper. Check the cake and use a spatula or large spoon to push down any uncooked cake mix into the bubbling mixture. Cook uncovered at full power for an additional 1–2 minutes, until cake mix is fully cooked. Be careful not to allow it to overcook, or the cake mix pieces will harden.

5   Cake should still be bubbling when finished. Let cool about 20 minutes before eating.

SLOW COOKER DUMP CAKES

———— •◦• ————

Not only can you make meals with your slow cooker, but you can make desserts too! I especially love slow cooker dump cakes because you don't have to constantly check on your cake.

You dump in all the ingredients, program the slow cooker, and then let it do the rest of the work, while you go off and get some work done. When you come back to your cake hours later, your cake is magically ready. It really takes the stress out of making a homemade dessert!

PUMPKIN CAKE

Prep time: 10–15 minutes Cook time: 3½ hours

Serves 9–12

Thanksgiving is such a stressful holiday for me because I usually cook the entire dinner myself. To make things a little easier on the day of the event, I try to make simple recipes or prepare dishes ahead of time. This slow cooker pumpkin cake is going on my Thanksgiving day menu next year. I love that I can just prep the ingredients and not worry about it again until after I've finished making everything else. The warm function on the slow cooker will keep the cake warm until it's time to serve!

2 cups (450 g) pumpkin purée

1 teaspoon (5 ml) cinnamon

1 cup (200 g) granulated white sugar

2 cups (320 g) Spice Cake Mix (page 19)

½ cup or 1 stick (4 ounces/113 g) unsalted butter, sliced into ¼-inch-thick (6 mm) squares

1 Lightly grease the bottom of a 6-quart (5.7 L) slow cooker. Dump and evenly spread pumpkin across bottom of slow cooker. Sprinkle pumpkin evenly first with cinnamon, then sugar.

2 Sprinkle dry cake mix evenly across slow cooker. Place butter slices evenly across top.

3 Cover your slow cooker and set it to cook for 3 hours on low heat. Cook for an additional 30 minutes, uncovered, on high heat.

4 Let cake cool for about 20 minutes before scooping out into individual dishes for serving. If desired, serve with a scoop of your favorite ice cream and/or any of the toppings provided on pages 168–173.

SALTED CARAMEL CHOCOLATE CAKE

Prep time: 10–15 minutes   Cook time: 4–4½ hours

Serves 9–12

This chocolate cake is mixed with salted caramel sauce. It remains gooey and pudding-like even after it's finished cooking.

1 cup (235 ml) lemon-lime soda (or the homemade version on page 173)

1 cup (155 g) Chocolate Cake Mix (page 18)

¼ cup (60 ml) salted caramel sauce

1   Lightly grease the bottom of a 6-quart (5.7 L) slow cooker.

2   Pour soda across bottom of slow cooker. Sprinkle evenly with dry cake mix. Drizzle caramel sauce across cake mix.

3   Cover your slow cooker and set it to cook for 4 hours on low heat. The surface of your cake should look done, but may have some condensation on it. If there is a lot of condensation, cook for an additional 30 minutes, uncovered, on low heat. If you don't have a slow cooker, preheat the oven to 350°F (175°C). Bake for 25–30 minutes. About 20 minutes in, quickly check the cake. Use a spatula or large wooden spoon to push down any uncooked cake mix into the bubbling mixture. Do not worry if this breaks the surface of the cake. Let the cake continue to bake for an additional 5–10 minutes.

4   Let cake cool for about 20 minutes before scooping out into individual dishes for serving. If desired, serve with a scoop of your favorite ice cream and/or any of the toppings provided on pages 168–173.

STRAWBERRY CRUMBLE

— ◆·◆·◆ —

Prep time: 10–15 minutes   Cook time: 4½ hours

Serves 9–12

Whole red strawberries give this cake such a festive look. Some of the berries even look like hearts on top of the cake. If you really want to get fancy, you can slice your berries in half lengthwise to make sure they are all heart-shaped!

2 cups (300 g) frozen hulled strawberries

1 tablespoon (15 ml) cornstarch

½ cup (100 g) granulated white sugar

2 cups (320 g) White Cake Mix (page 20)

½ cup or 1 stick (4 ounces/57 g) unsalted butter, sliced into ¼-inch-thick (6 mm) squares

1   Lightly grease the bottom of a 6-quart (5.7 L) slow cooker. Dump and evenly spread strawberries across bottom of slow cooker. Sprinkle strawberries with cornstarch, then sugar.

2   Sprinkle dry cake mix evenly across slow cooker. Place butter slices evenly across top.

3   Cover your slow cooker and set it to cook for 4 hours on low heat. Cook for an additional 30 minutes (still with cover on) on high heat until surface is dark golden brown. If you don't have a slow cooker, preheat the oven to 350°F (175°C). Bake for 25–30 minutes. About 20 minutes in, quickly check the cake. Use a spatula or large wooden spoon to push down any uncooked cake mix into the bubbling mixture. Do not worry if this breaks the surface of the cake. Let the cake continue to bake for an additional 5–10 minutes.

4   Let cake cool for about 20 minutes before scooping out into individual dishes for serving. If desired, serve with a scoop of your favorite ice cream and/or any of the toppings provided on pages 168–173.

DECADENT CHOCOLATE CAKE

Prep time: 10–15 minutes   Cook time: 4 hours

Serves 9–12

This rich chocolate cake has a gooey, pudding-like middle. Every bite of thick, melted chocolate sauce is a piece of heaven. I highly recommend you dish this into bowls and serve it with ice cream (if you haven't already been doing so for every other cake!).

¾ cup (175 ml) lemon-lime soda (or the homemade version on page 173)

1 cup (155 g) Chocolate Cake Mix (page 18)

2 tablespoons (1 ounce/28 g) unsalted butter, sliced into ¼-inch-thick (6 mm) squares

1   Lightly grease the bottom of a 6-quart (5.7 L) slow cooker.

2   Pour soda across bottom of slow cooker. Sprinkle dry cake mix evenly across slow cooker. Place butter slices evenly across top.

3   Cover your slow cooker and set it to cook for 4 hours on low heat. The surface of your cake should look done, but may have some condensation on it. If there is a lot of condensation, cook for an additional 30 minutes, uncovered, on low.

4   Let cake cool for about 20 minutes before scooping out into individual dishes for serving. If desired, serve with a scoop of your favorite ice cream and/or any of the toppings provided on pages 168–173.

BLUEBERRY COCONUT COBBLER

Prep time: 10–15 minutes   Cook time: 4½ hours

Serves 9–12

The classic blueberry cobbler is made even better with a layer of sweetened coconut flakes. Add a few ingredients into your slow cooker and then you can go off and get some errands in or check some things off of your to-do list. For a brown and crisper cobbler topping, cook for an additional 30 minutes on high heat after the cake is done cooking on low heat.

4 cups (620 g) frozen blueberries

2 tablespoons (30 ml) cornstarch

1 cup (200 g) granulated white sugar

2 cups (320 g) White Cake Mix (page 20)

1 cup (90 g) sweetened coconut flakes

½ cup or 1 stick (4 ounces/113 g) butter, sliced into ¼-inch-thick (6 mm) squares

1   Lightly grease the bottom of a 6-quart (5.7 L) slow cooker. Dump and spread blueberries evenly across the bottom. Sprinkle blueberries evenly first with cornstarch, then sugar.

2   Sprinkle dry cake mix evenly across the slow cooker. Scatter cake mix with coconut flakes. Spread butter slices evenly across top.

3   Cover your slow cooker and set it to cook for 4 hours on low heat. Cook for an additional 30 minutes at high heat to brown the top layer.

4   Let cake cool for about 20 minutes before scooping out into individual dishes for serving. If desired, serve with a scoop of your favorite ice cream and/or any of the toppings provided on pages 168–173.

CHERRY CHOCOLATE CAKE

Prep time: 10–15 minutes   Cook time: 4–4½ hours

Serves 9–12

Cherries and chocolate make a great pairing. Not only is the deep red color of cherries a beautiful color contrast with the dark brown chocolate, but the ingredients taste good together too. The sweet cherries also keep the chocolate layer from being too rich, making this a perfect choice if you're looking for a lighter chocolate dessert.

2 cups (310 g) frozen pitted cherries

1 tablespoon (15 ml) cornstarch

½ cup (100 g) granulated white sugar

1 cup (155 g) Chocolate Cake Mix (page 18)

¼ cup or ½ stick (2 ounces/57 g) unsalted butter, sliced into ¼-inch-thick (6 mm) squares

1 Lightly grease the bottom of a 6-quart (5.7 L) slow cooker.

2 Dump and evenly spread cherries across the bottom of slow cooker. Sprinkle cherries with cornstarch, then sugar.

3 Sprinkle dry cake mix evenly across slow cooker. Place butter slices evenly across top.

4 Cover your slow cooker and set it to cook for 4 hours on low heat. The surface of your cake should look done, but may have some condensation on it. If there is a lot of condensation, cook for an additional 30 minutes, uncovered, on low heat.

5 Let cake cool for about 20 minutes before scooping out into individual dishes for serving. If desired, serve with a scoop of your favorite ice cream and/or any of the toppings provided on pages 168–173.

SNACK DUMP CAKES

What exactly is a snack cake? I think of snack cakes as sweet treats that you can grab to eat on the go with your hands or that you can easily serve on a plate with a cup of tea or coffee. You can either snack on these sweets yourself or share with a group of friends or family.

COCONUT CAKE BARS

Prep time: 10–15 minutes   Cook time: 30–35 minutes

Serves 9–12

Do you love coconut? Do you love chewy desserts? If the answer to both questions is yes, then this cake is for you. These coconut cake bars are chock-full of coconut and have a light, chewy texture. I hope you enjoy them as much as I do!

½ cup (120 ml) sweetened condensed milk

1 cup (160 g) White Cake Mix (page 20)

½ cup (120 ml) lemon-lime soda (or the homemade version on page 173)

½ cup (45 g) sweetened coconut flakes

¼ cup or ½ stick (2 ounces/ 57 g) unsalted butter, sliced into ¼-inch-thick (6 mm) squares

1   Preheat oven to 350°F (175°C). Grease or line a 9 × 9-inch (23 × 23 cm) baking pan. If lining pan, grease bottom after lining it (see page 14).

2   Drizzle condensed milk evenly across bottom of pan. Sprinkle with dry cake mix. Drizzle soda evenly across cake mix; then sprinkle evenly with coconut flakes (covering entire surface). Spread butter slices evenly across top.

3   Bake for approximately 30–35 minutes, until the surface is golden brown. Because the coconut flakes are covering the entire cake surface, you should not need to push down any cake mix during the cooking process.

4   Let cake cool for about 15–20 minutes before cutting and serving.

GOOEY CAKE BARS

— • • • —

Prep time: 10–15 minutes   Cook time: 30–35 minutes

Serves 9–12

These thin, gooey bars are chewy, sticky, and sweet. They are fun to eat, even if a little messy. Just be sure to grab a couple of extra napkins!

2 tablespoons (30 ml) unsalted butter, melted

1 cup (160 g) White Cake Mix (page 20)

½ cup (120 ml) sweetened condensed milk

¼ cup (45 g) white chocolate chips

2 tablespoons (1 ounce/28 g) unsalted butter, sliced into ¼-inch-thick (6 mm) squares

1   Preheat oven to 350°F (175°C). Grease or line a 9 × 9-inch (23 × 23 cm) baking pan.

2   Drizzle melted butter evenly across bottom of pan. Sprinkle white cake mix evenly across pan. Drizzle condensed milk evenly across cake mix; then scatter white chocolate chips across pan. Spread butter slices evenly across top.

3   Bake for approximately 30–35 minutes, until surface is golden brown. About 20 minutes in, quickly check the cake. Use a spatula or large spoon to moisten any uncooked cake mix, spreading from the wet sections next to it. Do not worry if this breaks the surface of the cake. Let the cake continue to bake for an additional 5–10 minutes, until the surface is golden brown.

4   Let cake cool for about 15–20 minutes before cutting and serving.

CHOCOLATE CHIP COOKIE CAKE

Prep time: 10–15 minutes Cook time: 25–30 minutes

Serves 2

This recipe makes one extra-large cookie that you can remove from the baking dish and eat like a regular cookie, or you can also eat it right in the baking dish with a scoop of ice cream for the ultimate deep-dish cookie experience.

1 cup (240 ml) vanilla ice cream, melted

1 cup (160 g) White Cake Mix (page 20), sifted (see page 15)

¼ cup (45 g) semisweet chocolate chips

¼ cup or ½ stick (2 ounces/57 g) unsalted butter, melted

1 Preheat oven to 350°F (175°C). Grease a small round baking dish that measures about 5½ inches (14 cm) in diameter.

2 Pour melted ice cream across bottom of dish. Sift in cake mix.

3 Scatter chocolate chips over cake mix. Starting at the center of the dish, evenly pour in the melted butter.

4 Bake for approximately 25–30 minutes. About 20 minutes in, quickly check the cake. Use a spatula or large spoon to moisten any uncooked cake mix, spreading from the wet sections next to it. Do not worry if this breaks the surface of the cake. Let the cake continue to bake for an additional 5–10 minutes, until the surface is golden brown.

5 Let cake cool for about 10 minutes before removing from baking dish or adding ice cream to baking dish and serving.

JAM CAKE BARS

Prep time: 10–15 minutes   Cook time: 30–35 minutes

Serves 9–12

This cake really brings out the kid in me. With its thick layer of jam, this cake is a little bit like taking an entire jar of fresh-made jam and dipping your spoon in to eat it straight. The thin layer of buttery crumble makes it even better.

1 cup (235 ml) jam of your choice

1 cup (160 g) White Cake Mix (page 20)

¼ cup or ½ stick (2 ounces/57 g) unsalted butter, sliced into ¼-inch-thick (6 mm) squares

1 Preheat oven to 350°F (175°C). Grease or line a 9 × 9-inch (23 × 23 cm) baking pan.

2 Spread jam evenly across bottom of pan. Sprinkle dry cake mix evenly across jam. Place butter slices evenly across top.

3 Bake for about 30–35 minutes. About 25 minutes in, quickly check the cake. Use a spatula or large wooden spoon to push down any uncooked cake mix into the bubbling mixture. Do not worry if this breaks the surface of the cake. Let the cake continue to bake for an additional 5–10 minutes, until the surface is golden brown.

4 Let cake cool for about 15–20 minutes before cutting and serving.

CHOCOLATE CHOCOLATE-CHIP COOKIE CAKE

Prep time: 10–15 minutes   Cook time: 25–30 minutes

Serves 1

If you're a chocoholic, this recipe is for you! This cookie starts with a chocolate cookie base, and is then studded with chocolate chips for double the chocolate pleasure.

½ cup (120 ml) chocolate ice cream, melted

½ cup (78 g) Chocolate Cake Mix (page 18), sifted (see page 15)

2 tablespoons (30 ml) semisweet chocolate chips

2 tablespoons (1 ounce/28 g) unsalted butter, melted

1   Preheat oven to 350°F (175°C). Grease a small round baking dish that measures about 5½ inches (14 cm) in diameter.

2   Pour melted ice cream across bottom of dish. Sift in cake mix.

3   Scatter chocolate chips over cake mix. Starting at the center of the pan, evenly pour in the melted butter.

4   Bake for approximately 25–30 minutes. About 20 minutes in, quickly check the cake. Use a spatula or large spoon to moisten any uncooked cake mix, spreading from the wet sections next to it. Do not worry if this breaks the surface of the cake. Let the cake continue to bake for an additional 5–10 minutes, until the surface is golden brown.

5   Let cake cool for about 10 minutes before removing from baking dish or adding ice cream to baking dish and serving.

BLUEBERRY COOKIE CAKE

Prep time: 10–15 minutes   Cook time: 30–35 minutes

Serves 9–12

This recipe makes a large sheet of cookie cake, which can then be cut up and served as individual cookie bars. Since the recipe contains fresh blueberries, I'm going to pretend this qualifies as a healthy snack.

1 cup (235 ml) vanilla ice cream, melted

1 cup (160 g) White Cake mix (page 20), sifted (see page 15)

½ cup (75 g) fresh blueberries

¼ cup or ½ stick (2 ounces/57 g) unsalted butter, sliced into ¼-inch-thick (6 mm) squares

1   Preheat oven to 350°F (175°C). Grease or line a 9 × 9-inch (23 × 23 cm) baking pan.

2   Pour melted ice cream across bottom of pan. Evenly sift dry cake mix over ice cream; then scatter cake mix with blueberries. Spread butter slices evenly across top.

3   Bake for approximately 30–35 minutes. About 20 minutes in, quickly check the cake. Use a spatula or large wooden spoon to moisten any uncooked cake mix by spreading from any wet sections next to it. Do not worry if this breaks the surface of the cake. Let the cake continue to bake for an additional 10–15 minutes, until the surface is golden brown.

4   Let cake cool for about 15–20 minutes before removing from baking dish or adding ice cream to baking dish and serving.

PEANUT BUTTER AND JELLY CAKE BARS

Prep time: 10–15 minutes   **Cook time:** 30–35 minutes

Serves 9–12

These fun bars turn the ultimate children's sandwich into cake bar form. Of course it's not limited to just kids to enjoy. Do we ever really grow out of our love for peanut butter and jelly? I sure haven't!

1 cup (235 ml) jam of your choice

½ cup (130 g) peanut butter

1 cup (160 g) White Cake Mix (page 20)

¼ cup or ½ stick (2 ounces/57 g) unsalted butter, sliced into ¼-inch-thick (6 mm) squares

1 Preheat oven to 350°F (175°C). Grease or line a 9 × 9-inch (23 × 23 cm) baking pan.

2 Spread jam evenly across bottom of pan. Add 1 teaspoon dollops of peanut butter across jam. Sprinkle with dry cake mix. Spread butter slices evenly across top.

3 Bake for about 30–35 minutes. About 25 minutes in, quickly check the cake. Use a spatula or large wooden spoon to push down any uncooked cake mix into the bubbling mixture. Do not worry if this breaks the surface of the cake. Let the cake continue to bake for an additional 5–10 minutes, until the surface is golden brown.

4 Let cake cool for about 20–30 minutes before cutting and serving.

HOLIDAY DUMP CAKES

—— •◆• ——

This chapter contains dump cakes perfect for many major food-oriented holidays, from birthdays to Thanksgiving. You can make these cakes for the special occasion itself or as a way of using up leftover amounts of popular holiday ingredients like pumpkin and cranberries.

BIRTHDAY SPRINKLES CAKE

─ • ◆ • ─

Prep time: 10–15 minutes   Cook time: 25–30 minutes

Serves 1

Sometimes you don't want the fuss of an entire cake. I'm finding that the older I get, the less attention I want drawn to my birthday. When did I get this old?! This little cake is a great way to commemorate the day without too much commotion. Stick a candle in the middle and make a wish!

¼ cup (60 ml) lemon-lime soda (or the homemade version on page 173)

½ cup (80 g) Funfetti Cake Mix (page 19), sifted (see page 15)

1 teaspoon (5 ml) sprinkles

2 tablespoons (1 ounce/28 g) unsalted butter, melted

1   Preheat oven to 350°F (175°C). Grease a small round baking dish that measures about 5 ½ inches (14 cm) in diameter.

2   Pour soda across bottom of dish. Sift in cake mix.

3   Scatter sprinkles across cake mix. Starting at the center of the dish, evenly pour in the melted butter.

4   Bake for approximately 25–30 minutes. About 20–25 minutes in, quickly check the cake. Use a spatula or large spoon to push down any uncooked cake mix into the bubbling mixture. Do not worry if this breaks the surface of the cake. Let the cake continue to bake for an additional 5 minutes, until the surface is golden brown.

5   Let cake cool for about 10 minutes before serving. If desired, serve with a scoop of your favorite ice cream and/or any of the toppings provided on pages 168–173.

S'MORE CAKE

— ◆ —

Prep time: 10–15 minutes   Cook time: 20–25 minutes

Serves 9–12

No need to start a bonfire to enjoy these treats! These cookie cake bars have chocolate squares, pieces of graham crackers, and toasted marshmallows—just like s'mores!

1 cup (160 g) White Cake Mix (page 20)

¼ cup or ½ stick (2 ounces/57 g) unsalted butter, sliced into ¼-inch-thick (6 mm) squares

9 1¾ inch (4.5 cm) chocolate squares (such as individual Ghirardelli squares)

1 cup (50 g) mini marshmallows

2 sheets graham crackers, lightly broken up

1 Preheat oven to 350°F (175°C). Grease or line a 9 × 9-inch (23 × 23 cm) baking pan. If lining pan, grease bottom after lining it (see page 14).

2 Sprinkle cake mix evenly across bottom of pan. Spread butter slices evenly across cake mix. Place chocolate squares evenly across. Scatter marshmallows and graham cracker pieces.

3 Bake for about 20–25 minutes, until top of the cake is a dark golden brown and cake mix underneath is cooked.

4 Let cake cool for about 20 minutes before cutting and serving.

CRANBERRY COBBLER

Prep time: 10–15 minutes   Cook time: 30–35 minutes

Serves 9–12

This dessert works both as a unique Thanksgiving dessert and a way to use up leftover cranberry sauce. Since cranberry sauce takes a long time to make from scratch, I use canned cranberry sauce with whole berries for this recipe.

1 14-ounce (397 g) can cranberry sauce with whole cranberries

1 cup (160 g) White Cake Mix (page 20)

¼ cup or ½ stick (2 ounces/57 g) unsalted butter, sliced into ¼-inch-thick (6 mm) squares

1   Preheat oven to 350°F (175°C). Grease or line a 9 × 9-inch (23 × 23 cm) baking pan.

2   Spread cranberry sauce evenly across bottom of pan. Sprinkle cranberry sauce with dry cake mix. Spread butter slices evenly across top.

3   Bake for about 30–35 minutes. About 25 minutes in, quickly check the cake. Use a spatula or large spoon to push down any uncooked cake mix into the bubbling mixture. Do not worry if this breaks the surface of the cake. Let the cake continue to bake for an additional 5–10 minutes, until the surface is golden brown.

4   Let cake cool about 20 minutes before scooping into dishes and serving. If desired, serve with a scoop of your favorite ice cream and/or any of the toppings provided on pages 168–173.

PUMPKIN CHOCOLATE CHIP CAKE

—— • • • ——

Prep time: 10–15 minutes   Cook time: 35–40 minutes

Serves 9–12

For another unique dessert option at Thanksgiving dinner, try this sweet pumpkin cobbler cake that is studded with chocolate chips. It's easier to make than pumpkin pie or pumpkin bread, but equally as delicious.

1 cup (225 g) canned pumpkin purée

½ cup (100 g) granulated white sugar

½ cup (80 g) Spice Cake Mix (page 19)

¼ cup (45 g) semisweet chocolate chips

¼ cup or ½ stick (2 ounces/57 g) unsalted butter, sliced into ¼-inch-thick (6 mm) squares

1   Preheat oven to 350°F (175°C). Grease or line a 9 × 9-inch (23 × 23 cm) baking pan.

2   Evenly spread pumpkin purée across bottom of pan. Sprinkle with sugar.

3   Evenly sprinkle dry cake mix across pan. Scatter with chocolate chips. Spread butter slices evenly across top.

4   Bake for 35–40 minutes. About 25 minutes in, quickly check the cake. Use a spatula or large wooden spoon to push down any uncooked cake mix into the bubbling mixture. Do not worry if this breaks the surface of the cake. Let the cake continue to bake for an additional 10–15 minutes, until the surface is dark golden brown.

5   Let cake cool for about 20–30 minutes before serving as the fruit layer will be extremely hot. If desired, serve with a scoop of your favorite ice cream and/or any of the toppings provided on pages 168–173.

CANDY BAR CAKE

— ● ● ● —

Prep time: 10–15 minutes   Cook time: 30–35 minutes

Serves 9–12

This cake is like a candy bar in cake form. It starts with chocolate cake mix and is topped with toffee bits, caramel sauce, chocolate syrup, chocolate chips, and chopped almonds. It's super sweet and yet quite delicious.

¼ cup (60 ml) lemon-lime soda (or the homemade version on page 173)

2 tablespoons (30 ml) caramel sauce

1 cup (155 g) Chocolate Cake Mix (page 18)

¼ cup (60 g) baking toffee pieces

¼ cup (45 g) semisweet chocolate chips

¼ cup (31 g) chopped almonds

2 tablespoons (30 ml) chocolate syrup

¼ cup or ½ stick (2 ounces/57 g) unsalted butter, sliced into ¼-inch-thick (6 mm) squares

1   Preheat oven to 350°F (175°C). Grease or line a 9 × 9-inch (23 × 23 cm) baking pan. If lining the pan, grease the bottom after you line it (see page 14).

2   Pour soda across bottom of pan. Drizzle caramel sauce evenly across pan. Sprinkle dry cake mix. Scatter toffee, chocolate chips, and almonds across cake mix. Drizzle with chocolate syrup. Spread butter slices evenly across pan.

3   Bake for about 30–35 minutes. About 25 minutes in, quickly check the cake. Use a spatula or large spoon to moisten any uncooked cake mix, spreading from the wet sections next to it. Do not worry if this breaks the surface of the cake. Let the cake continue to bake for an additional 5–10 minutes, until the cake mix looks completely cooked.

4   Let cake cool about 20 minutes before serving. If desired, serve with a scoop of your favorite ice cream and/or any of the toppings provided on pages 168–173.

EGGNOG CAKE

— ◆●◆ —

Prep time: 10–15 minutes   Cook time: 30–35 minutes

Serves 9–12

This chewy cake is a fun way to use up leftover eggnog. You can also serve it with a cup of eggnog for twice the eggnog enjoyment this holiday season!

1 cup (235 ml) spiced light
    eggnog, divided

1 cup (160 g) White Cake Mix
    (page 20), sifted (see
    page 15)

¼ cup or ½ stick (2 ounces/57 g)
    unsalted butter, sliced into
    ¼-inch-thick (6 mm) squares

1 Preheat oven to 350°F (175°C). Grease or line a 9 × 9-inch (23 × 23 cm) baking pan. If lining pan, grease bottom after lining it (see page 14).

2 Pour ¼ cup (60 ml) eggnog across bottom of pan. Sprinkle eggnog with dry cake mix. Pour remaining ¾ cup (175 ml) eggnog evenly across cake mix. Spread butter slices evenly across top.

3 Bake for about 30–35 minutes. About 25 minutes in, quickly check the cake. Use a spatula or large wooden spoon to push down any uncooked cake mix into the bubbling mixture. Do not worry if this breaks the surface of the cake. Let the cake continue to bake for an additional 5–10 minutes, until the surface is golden brown.

4 Let cake cool about 20 minutes before serving. If desired, serve with a scoop of your favorite ice cream and/or any of the toppings provided on pages 168–173.

MASHED SWEET POTATO CAKE

Prep time: 10–15 minutes   Cook time: 35–40 minutes

Serves 9–12

Canned mashed sweet potatoes are usually available around Thanksgiving, though you can also make your own by puréeing leftover roasted sweet potatoes. Either way, this makes a delicious belly-warming side or dessert during the Thanksgiving season.

1 cup (255 g) canned mashed sweet potatoes

½ cup (100 g) granulated white sugar

½ cup (80 g) Spice Cake Mix (page 19)

¼ cup or ½ stick (2 ounces/57 g) unsalted butter, sliced into ¼-inch-thick (6 mm) squares

1   Preheat oven to 350°F (175°C). Grease or line a 9 × 9-inch (23 × 23 cm) baking pan.

2   Evenly spread sweet potato across bottom of pan. Sprinkle sweet potatoes evenly with sugar.

3   Sprinkle dry cake mix evenly across pan. Spread butter slices evenly across top.

4   Bake for 35–40 minutes. About 25 minutes in, quickly check the cake. Use a spatula or large spoon to push down any uncooked cake mix into the bubbling mixture. Do not worry if this breaks the surface of the cake. Let the cake continue to bake for an additional 10–15 minutes, until the surface is dark golden brown.

5   Let cake cool for about 20–30 minutes before serving. If desired, serve with a scoop of your favorite ice cream and/or any of the toppings provided on pages 168–173.

FANCY DUMP CAKES

They say you should save the best for last, and it just so happens that this last chapter contains some of my favorite cakes. Many of these cakes contain alcohol, making them more suitable for an adults-only audience. These cakes are perfect for a dinner party, celebration, or other special occasion.

DULCE DE LECHE CHOCOLATE CAKE

— • • • —

Prep time: 10–15 minutes   Cook time: 30–35 minutes

Serves 12–15

Dulce de leche is a thick, caramelized milk sauce that literally translates to "candy made of milk." Doesn't that translation alone sound amazing? Dulce de leche is drizzled throughout this chocolate cake, which really takes it to the next level. You can usually find dulce de leche in the baking aisle, near the condensed milk.

¼ cup (60 ml) lemon-lime soda (or the homemade version on page 173)

½ cup (120 ml) dulce de leche sauce, divided

1 cup (155 g) Chocolate Cake Mix (page 18), sifted (see page 15)

¼ cup or ½ stick (2 ounces/57 g) unsalted butter, sliced into ¼-inch-thick (6 mm) squares

1 Preheat oven to 350°F (175°C). Grease or line a 9 × 9-inch (23 × 23 cm) baking pan. If lining baking pan, make sure to also grease the bottom after lining it (see page 14).

2 Pour soda across bottom of pan. Drizzle in ¼ cup (60 ml) dulce de leche.

3 Sift dry cake mix evenly across pan; then drizzle with remaining ¼ cup dulce de leche. Spread butter slices evenly across top.

4 Bake for 30–35 minutes. About 25 minutes in, quickly check the cake. Use a spatula or large spoon to moisten any uncooked cake mix, by spreading from wet sections next to it. Do not worry if this breaks the surface of the cake. Let the cake continue to bake for an additional 5–10 minutes, until all cake mix looks cooked.

5 Let cake cool for about 20 minutes to allow it to set before serving. If desired, serve with a scoop of your favorite ice cream and/or any of the toppings provided on pages 168–173.

BANANAS FOSTER CAKE

Prep time: 10–15 minutes   Cook time: 30–35 minutes

Serves 9–12

Originating in New Orleans, bananas Foster is a dessert made with bananas cooked in butter, cinnamon, and rum and then flambéed before being topped with ice cream. I was very fortunate to get the full tableside experience at Brennan's, where the dessert was first introduced, during my trip to New Orleans a few years ago. Since then I've been a little obsessed with it.

This dump cake does a stellar job of recreating all the flavors of a classic bananas Foster dessert, while also adding a nontraditional but delicious buttery crumble. Since the original is served with vanilla ice cream, I recommend that you do the same.

2 very ripe medium bananas, peeled and cut into ¼-inch-thick (6 mm) slices

2 tablespoons (30 ml) unsalted butter, melted

½ teaspoon (2.5 ml) ground nutmeg

¼ teaspoon (1.25 ml) ground cinnamon

¼ cup (60 ml) dark rum

¼ cup (60 g) light brown sugar, packed

1 cup (160 g) White Cake Mix (page 20)

¼ cup or ½ stick (2 ounces/57 g) unsalted butter, sliced into ¼-inch-thick (6 mm) squares

1. Preheat oven to 350°F (175°C). Grease or line a 9 × 9-inch (23 × 23 cm) baking pan.

2. Lay banana slices evenly across bottom of pan. You should have enough to line the entire bottom layer, with the slices side by side and touching, and then enough left over for a more spread-out layer on top.

3. Pour melted butter evenly across bananas. Sprinkle bananas evenly with nutmeg, then cinnamon. Drizzle rum across bananas; then sprinkle them with sugar. Sprinkle dry cake mix evenly across top. Spread butter slices evenly across top.

4. Bake for about 30–35 minutes. About 25 minutes in, quickly check the cake. Use a spatula or large spoon to push down any uncooked cake mix into the bubbling mixture. Do not worry if this breaks the surface of the cake. Let the cake continue to bake for an additional 5–10 minutes, until the surface is golden brown.

5. Let cake cool for about 20 minutes before cutting and serving with a scoop of vanilla ice cream.

POACHED PEARS CAKE

Prep time: 10–15 minutes   Cook time: 40–45 minutes
Serves 9–12

Pears are cooked in white wine and then topped with a buttery crumble for a very grown-up version of fruit crumble. The cake comes out a beautiful golden brown, giving it an elegant finished appearance.

1 15-ounce (425 g) can sliced pears in their own juices, drained and 3 tablespoons (45 ml) of juice reserved

1 tablespoon (15 ml) cornstarch

¼ cup (60 ml) white wine

¼ cup (50 g) granulated white sugar

1 cup (160 g) White Cake Mix (page 20)

¼ cup or ½ stick (2 ounces/57 g) unsalted butter, sliced into ¼-inch-thick (6 mm) squares

1   Preheat oven to 350°F (175°C). Grease or line a 9 × 9-inch (23 × 23 cm) baking pan.

2   Spread pear slices on their sides evenly across bottom of pan. Add in the reserved juice. Sprinkle pears evenly with cornstarch. Drizzle with white wine. Sprinkle pears with sugar, then dry cake mix. Spread butter slices evenly across top.

3   Bake for about 40–45 minutes. About 25 minutes in, quickly check the cake. Use a spatula or large spoon to push down any uncooked cake mix into the bubbling mixture. Do not worry if this breaks the surface of the cake. Let the cake continue to bake for an additional 15–20 minutes, until the surface is golden brown.

4   Let cake cool for about 20 minutes before serving. If desired, serve with a scoop of your favorite ice cream and/or any of the toppings provided on pages 168–173.

TURTLE CAKE

Prep time: 10–15 minutes   Cook time: 30–35 minutes

Serves 9–12

Chocolate cake is topped with caramel sauce and pecans, inspired by the popular confectionary treat. There's a sweet, gooey surprise in every bite.

¼ cup (60 ml) lemon-lime soda (or homemade version on page 173)

½ cup (120 ml) thick caramel sauce, divided

1 cup (155 g) Chocolate Cake Mix (page 18), sifted (see page 15)

¼ cup (60 ml) sweetened condensed milk

¼ cup (25 g) chopped pecans

¼ cup or ½ stick (2 ounces/57 g) unsalted butter, sliced into ¼-inch-thick (6 mm) squares

1 Preheat oven to 350°F (175°C). Grease or line a 9 × 9-inch (23 × 23 cm) baking pan. If lining baking pan, make sure to also grease parchment paper after lining it (see page 14).

2 Pour soda across bottom of pan. Drizzle in ¼ cup (60 ml) caramel sauce. Sift dry cake mix evenly across pan. Drizzle ¼ cup (60 ml) condensed milk across cake mix; then sprinkle with pecans. Drizzle remaining ¼ cup (60 ml) caramel sauce over cake. Spread butter slices evenly across top.

3 Bake for 30–35 minutes. About 25 minutes in, quickly check the cake. Use a spatula or large spoon to moisten any uncooked cake mix, by spreading from wet sections next to it. Do not continue to bake for an additional 5–10 minutes, until all cake mix looks cooked. It is okay to remove the cake from the oven even though it is still bubbling.

4 Let cake cool for about 20 minutes before serving. If desired, serve with a scoop of your favorite ice cream and/or any of the toppings provided on pages 168–173.

CHERRIES JUBILEE CAKE

Prep time: 10–15 minutes   Cook time: 30–35 minutes

Serves 9–12

Cherries jubilee is traditionally made with cherries soaked in liqueur, which are then flambéed and topped with ice cream. Similarly, this cake has rum-soaked cherries, which are then cooked and topped with a buttery crumble. No flambéing required!

2 cups (310 g) frozen pitted cherries

1 tablespoon (15 ml) cornstarch

¾ cup (150 g) granulated white sugar

¼ cup (60 ml) dark rum

1 cup (155 g) Chocolate Cake Mix (page 18)

¼ cup or ½ stick (2 ounces/57 g) unsalted butter, sliced into ¼-inch-thick (6 mm) squares

1. Preheat oven to 350°F (175°C). Grease or line a 9 × 9-inch (23 × 23 cm) baking pan.

2. Dump and spread cherries evenly across bottom of pan. Sprinkle cherries with cornstarch, then sugar. Drizzle cherries with rum. Sprinkle dry cake mix evenly across pan. Spread butter slices evenly across top.

3. Bake for about 30–35 minutes. About 25 minutes in, quickly check the cake. Use a spatula or large wooden spoon to push down any uncooked cake mix into the bubbling mixture. Do not worry if this breaks the surface of the cake. Let the cake continue to bake for an additional 5–10 minutes, until cake mix looks completely cooked.

4. Let cake cool for about 20 minutes before cutting and serving with a scoop of ice cream.

WHITE CHOCOLATE RASPBERRY CAKE

Prep time: 10–15 minutes   Cook time: 30–35 minutes

Serves 9–12

White chocolate and raspberries always seem to appear together in fancy settings. I don't know if it's because garnishing desserts with red raspberries immediately elevates their appearance or because many people don't really appreciate raspberries until they become an adult. Either way, they make a delicious pairing and add a beautiful color to this elegant dessert.

2 cups (500 g) frozen raspberries

1 tablespoon (15 ml) cornstarch

½ cup (100 g) granulated white sugar

1 cup (160 g) White Cake Mix (page 20)

¼ cup (45 g) white chocolate chips

¼ cup or ½ stick (2 ounces/57 g) unsalted butter, sliced into ¼-inch-thick (6 mm) squares

1   Preheat oven to 350°F (175°C). Grease or line a 9 × 9-inch (23 × 23 cm) baking pan.

2   Dump and spread raspberries evenly across bottom of pan. Sprinkle raspberries evenly with cornstarch, then sugar.

3   Sprinkle dry cake mix evenly across pan. Scatter chocolate chips evenly across cake mix. Spread butter slices evenly across top.

4   Bake for 30–35 minutes. About 25 minutes in, quickly check the cake. Use a spatula or large wooden spoon to push down any uncooked cake mix into the bubbling mixture. Do not worry if this breaks the surface of the cake. Let the cake continue to bake for an additional 5–10 minutes, until the surface is golden brown.

5   Let cake cool for about 20–30 minutes before serving. If desired, serve with a scoop of your favorite ice cream and/or any of the toppings provided on pages 168–173.

SKINNY DUMP CAKES

Maybe it's your New Year's resolution to cut down on calories or you want to lose a few pounds before a big event. Or maybe you try to maintain a healthy lifestyle but still want the occasional treat. These skinny dump cakes will satisfy your sweet tooth without causing you to fall off your diet.

MANGO CRUMBLE

Prep time: 10–15 minutes   Cook time: 35–40 minutes

Serves 8

About 87 calories per serving

In this crumble, we're reducing the buttery crumble topping slightly and letting the naturally sweet mangoes be the star. Yes, it tastes lighter, but your body will thank you later.

1½ cups (262 g) frozen mango chunks

1 tablespoon (15 ml) cornstarch

2 tablespoons (30 ml) granulated white sugar

½ cup (80 g) White Cake Mix (page 20)

¼ cup (120 ml) lemon-lime soda (or the homemade version on page 173)

1 tablespoon (½ ounce/14 g) unsalted butter, divided into 4 even squares

1 Preheat oven to 350°F (175°C). Grease or line a 9 × 9-inch (23 × 23 cm) baking pan.

2 Dump and evenly spread mango across pan. Sprinkle mangoes with cornstarch, then sugar. Sprinkle dry cake mix evenly across pan. Pour soda across the surface of the cake mix. Place butter squares evenly across top.

3 Bake for about 35–40 minutes. About 20 minutes in, quickly check the cake. Use a spatula or large wooden spoon to push down any uncooked cake mix into the liquid mixture. Do not worry if this breaks the surface of the cake. Let the cake continue to bake for an additional 15–20 minutes, until the surface is light golden brown.

4 Let cake cool for about 20 minutes before serving.

RASPBERRY CLOUD CAKE

Prep time: 10–15 minutes   Cook time: 30–35 minutes

Serves 9

About 38 calories per serving

On page 84, I introduced a cloud-like cake made with angel food cake mix. This is a full-sized variation of that dessert, in case you want to share this delightful cake with your friends. Because angel food cake is made predominantly of egg whites, this cake is very low in calories, but very delicious.

Remember, this cake needs to be consumed right away. It will puff up when baking, but will sink down soon after and turn gooey once it begins to cool.

1 cup (125 g) fresh raspberries

1 cup (120 g) store-bought angel food cake mix

1 cup (235 ml) club soda

1   Preheat oven to 350°F (175°C). Grease or line a 9 × 9-inch (23 × 23 cm) baking pan.

2   Dump and spread berries across bottom of pan. Sprinkle dry cake mix over berries.

3   Gently pour soda over surface of the cake. The club soda should develop a thick foam. If there is any cake mix not covered in foam, gently move it with a spatula until all cake mix is completely covered.

4   Bake for approximately 30–35 minutes. The top of the cake should be lightly toasted brown and the edges of the cake should no longer look gooey. Let cake cool for a few minutes before eating right away.

APPLESAUCE CAKE

Prep time: 10–15 minutes   Cook time: 4–4½ hours

Serves 9

About 82 calories per serving

To lighten up this cake, applesauce is used for the fruit layer. Diet soda replaces butter to cook the cake mix without all the calories. This cake will be soft rather than crunchy and buttery, but it will still satisfy your sweet tooth.

1½ cups (370 g) unsweetened applesauce

1 cup (160 g) White Cake Mix (page 20)

½ cup (120 ml) lemon-lime soda (or the homemade version on page 173)

1   Lightly grease bottom of 6-quart slow cooker. Spread applesauce evenly across bottom.

2   Sprinkle cake mix evenly across applesauce. Pour soda evenly across cake mix.

3   Cover your slow cooker and set it to cook for 4 hours on low heat. After 4 hours, your cake should look done; however the surface may have some condensation. If it does, cook for additional 30 minutes, uncovered, on low heat.

4   Let cake cool for about 20 minutes before scooping out into individual dishes for serving.

PINEAPPLE CRISP

Prep time: 10–15 minutes   Cook time: 30–35 minutes

Serves 7

About 118 calories per serving

This is a lightened-up version of a traditional crisp. Pineapples have a wonderful natural sweetness to them that really shines through, and their juices coat the oats in the process too.

2 cups (362 g) canned pineapple chunks in natural pineapple juices, drained and ½ cup (120 ml) juice reserved

1 tablespoon (15 ml) cornstarch

1 cup (80 g) quick oats

2 tablespoons (1 ounce/28 g) unsalted butter, melted

1. Preheat oven to 350°F (175°C). Grease or line a 9 × 9-inch (23 × 23 cm) baking pan.

2. Dump and evenly spread pineapples and reserved juice across pan. Sprinkle pineapples with cornstarch.

3. Sprinkle oats evenly across pan. Pour butter evenly across oats.

4. Bake for about 30–35 minutes, until pineapple juices have thickened and oats are fully cooked.

5. Let cake cool for about 20 minutes before serving as the fruit layer will be extremely hot.

CHOCOLATE GANACHE

1 cup (120 g) heavy cream

8 ounces (226 g) bittersweet or semisweet chocolate, chopped

1. Add heavy cream to a small saucepan and bring to a boil. Turn off heat and immediately add chopped chocolate.

2. Whisk until chocolate is completely melted and smooth. Drizzle over desserts while ganache is still warm. Once fully cooled, ganache will stiffen. Any unused ganache can be poured into a container, sealed, and stored in refrigerator for up to one week. Ganache will harden in the fridge, but can be reheated on the stove or in the microwave and whisked until smooth.

CHOCOLATE SYRUP

1 cup (96 g) unsweetened
  Dutch process cocoa powder

1 cup (200 g) granulated
  white sugar

¼ teaspoon (1.25 ml) salt

1 cup (235 ml) water

1 teaspoon (5 ml) vanilla extract

1 Whisk cocoa powder, sugar, and salt together in a small bowl. In a medium saucepan over medium heat, add water and vanilla. Slowly whisk in the cocoa mixture until mixture becomes smooth.

2 Bring mixture to a gentle boil. Stir continuously for about 5 minutes or until thickened. Syrup will thicken further once cooled, so it is okay if it still a little thin after 5 minutes.

3 If syrup is being used immediately, use it while warm. If it is being made ahead of time for use later on, pour syrup into a jar while it is still warm and seal. Store syrup in refrigerator for up to one month. Bring to room temperature before using.

CREAM CHEESE FROSTING

— ◆ ◆ —

1 cup or 2 sticks (8 ounces/226 g) unsalted butter

8 ounces (130 g) cream cheese

2 cups (240 g) powdered sugar

1 teaspoon (5 ml) vanilla extract

1. Combine all ingredients in a mixing bowl and mix on high speed with a mixer (either hand-held or a stand mixer) until smooth and fluffy.

2. Use immediately. Any unused frosting can be stored in a sealed container in the refrigerator, for up to three days.

MASCARPONE FROSTING

— ◆ ◆ —

8 ounces (227 g) mascarpone cheese

½ cup (60 g) powdered sugar

1 cup (120 g) heavy cream

1. Add all ingredients into a medium mixing bowl. Beat with mixer at high speed for a few minutes until stiff peaks form.

2. For best results, use immediately. Store any unused frosting in a sealed container in the refrigerator for up to three days.

WHIPPED CREAM

2 cups (240 g) heavy cream

⅜ cup (75 g) granulated white sugar

1 Add ingredients to a mixing bowl. Beat with a mixer on high speed for a few minutes until stiff peaks form.

2 Serve immediately. Whipped cream is best used right away or it will start to turn runny over time. You can store any unused whipped cream in a sealed container in the refrigerator for up to three days, but the consistency may not be as thick as fresh whipped cream.

SALTED CARAMEL SAUCE

1 cup (240 g) light brown sugar, packed

¼ cup or ½ stick (2 ounces/57 g) salted butter

½ cup (60 g) heavy cream

1 teaspoon (5 ml) vanilla extract

1 pinch salt

1 Add all ingredients into a medium saucepan and cook over medium heat, bringing to a gentle boil. Lower heat if needed to keep the sauce at a gentle boil.

2 Whisk continuously while cooking for about 7 minutes, until thickened.

3 Serve right away. Store any unused sauce in a tightly sealed jar in the refrigerator for up to two weeks.

DAIRY-FREE COCONUT WHIPPED CREAM

---

1 14-ounce (414 ml) can full-fat coconut milk or coconut cream*

1–3 tablespoons (8 g–24 g) powdered sugar

1 Place coconut milk can in refrigerator to chill overnight, or for at least 12 hours. Right before making coconut whipped cream, remove can from fridge. This should cause the cream and liquid to separate, with the cream floating on top and the liquid at the bottom. For easy extraction, flip can over before opening it. This way the liquid will be on top when you open the can. Carefully pour out this liquid, to be used in something else.

2 Add coconut cream to a mixing bowl. Add sugar in 1 tablespoon increments. The sugar amount needed will vary depending on the brand of coconut milk used. Mix on high speed with a mixer until soft peaks form.

3 Use immediately. Coconut cream is best used right away as it will lose its consistency and become runny over time. However, if you do have any unused cream, store in the refrigerator in a sealed container for up to three days.

* *For best results, I recommend coconut cream. I usually use Trader Joe's brand, but you can find other brands at supermarkets and on Amazon. Coconut cream is already much thicker to start with and will thicken further in the refrigerator. One can of coconut cream will also yield much more cream than one can of coconut milk. Full fat (not light!) coconut milk also works, but results can be inconsistent depending on the brand. I also found that some brands I used to like changed their formula and suddenly didn't work for me anymore. Currently, the brand I've had the most success with is Whole Foods.*

VANILLA GLAZE

1 cup (120 g) powdered sugar

¼ teaspoon (1.25 ml) vanilla extract

1–2 tablespoons (15 ml–30 ml) milk

1 In a small bowl, add sugar, vanilla and 1 tablespoon milk. Whisk until smooth.

2 If glaze is too thick, add more milk, 1 teaspoon at a time. Whisk after each addition until the glaze is smooth and your desired consistency.

3 Drizzle over desserts. Store any unused glaze in a sealed container in the refrigerator for up to three days. Glaze will harden in the refrigerator and will need to be heated briefly on the stove or in the microwave before reusing.

LEMON-LIME SODA SUBSTITUTE

¼ cup (60 ml) club soda

2 teaspoons (10 ml) granulated white sugar

1 Stir together the club soda (from a freshly opened can) and sugar until dissolved. Use soda substitute immediately in the recipe that calls for soda.

* This soda substitute is not meant to be made ahead of time and stored, nor is it a homemade recipe for soda. Instead, it is a quick fix for recipes that require soda, when you don't have or don't want to use a commercial soda. You don't need to add lemon or lime flavoring because that flavor in commercial soda disappears during baking anyway. Most of the recipes that require soda call for ¼ cup (60 ml), which is the amount this recipe makes. If a recipe calls for other amounts, please double or adjust as needed.

INDEX

—◦•◦—